A WORLD OF POETRY

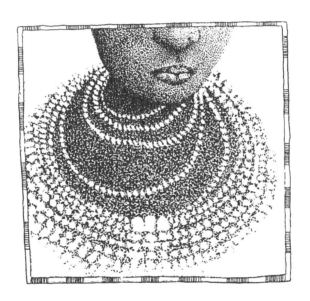

SELECTED BY MICHAEL ROSEN

Kingfisher

KINGFISHER
An imprint of Larousse plc
Elsley House, 24-30 Great Titchfield Street
London W1P 7AD

This edition published by Kingfisher 1995
First published in paperback by Kingfisher 1993
2 4 6 8 10 9 7 5 3 1 (hardback)
2 4 6 8 10 9 7 5 3 (paperback)
First published in hardback by Kingfisher 1991

A CIP catalogue record for this book
is available from the British Library

ISBN 1 85697 480 4 (hardback)
ISBN 1 85697 221 6 (paperback)

Printed and bound in Great Britain by
BPC Paperbacks Ltd
A Member of
The British Printing Company Ltd

CONTENTS

INTRODUCTION

If I say to you "Once upon a time . . ." you expect me to tell you a story. If I say to you "In Paris today, three masked men approached a . . ." you probably think I'm pretending to be a newsreader. If I say "Stir in the milk until the mixture is wet . . ." it's a recipe. In other words, you can guess what wavelength I'm on after only a few words.

But what about poetry? Sometimes you can guess the wavelength after a few words but other times you've got to stick with it for a bit longer. It's a bit like when you switch on a TV programme in the middle and you spend a few minutes trying to figure out what's going on – why are they laughing at the tall guy with the hat?

So why is poetry like this? Why isn't all of it as easy as "Once upon a time"? Sometimes it's because it was written a long time ago and people spoke and wrote differently then. Sometimes it's because it comes from a different country or culture and you don't think in quite the same way as that writer. Sometimes it's because over hundreds of years people who write poetry have developed their own ways of going on – their equivalents of "Once upon a time" or "Stir in the milk" – and you don't recognize them. So the trick with poetry is to be patient, let it happen slowly, maybe ask someone to help you, and then what seemed like an impossible puzzle might turn out to be a fascinating glimpse of how other people think.

In actual fact, I think most of the poems you'll find in this book will talk to you straightaway about things that are mysterious, funny, horrific, sad, wild, ugly, calm, wonderful, and any other feeling you may have. We've called the book 'A World of Poetry' because that's what it is: a world of thoughts and feelings, images and ideas collected from all over the world and spreading over thousands of years. The poems are *by* many kinds of people, so I hope this book is *for* many kinds of people.

Michael Rosen

SLAVERY

Got one mind for the boss to see,
Got another mind for what I know is me.

AFRO-AMERICAN

DON'T CALL ALLIGATOR LONG-MOUTH
TILL YOU CROSS RIVER

Call alligator long-mouth
call alligator saw-mouth
call alligator pushy-mouth
call alligator scissors-mouth
call alligator raggedy-mouth
call alligator bumpy-bum
call alligator all dem rude word
but better wait
    till you cross river.

JOHN AGARD

ONE QUESTION FROM A BULLET

I want to give up being a bullet
I've been a bullet too long

I want to be an innocent coin
in the hand of a child
and be squeezed through the slot
of a bubblegum machine

I want to give up being a bullet
I've been a bullet too long

I want to be a good luck seed
lying idle in somebody's pocket
or some ordinary little stone
on the way to becoming an earring
or just lying there unknown
among a crowd of other ordinary stones

I want to give up being a bullet
I've been a bullet too long

The question is
Can you give up being a killer?

JOHN AGARD

MY BABY BROTHER

My baby brother is a killer
He pulls my hair and throws me down
on the floor and spits in my face and
squeezes my nose and takes off my
glasses and then tries them on and
throws them away and he jumps on
my stomach and he bites my toes and
he counts my fingers and my mother
says, "Ian get off the floor".

IAN AITKEN

BITTER

If you were to squeeze me and wash,
squeeze me and wash,
squeeze and wash me,
and I foam,
again and again,
like bitter-leaf
left out too long to wither,
you would not squeeze
the bitterness out of me.

IFI AMADIUME

THE FLOOD

Now I will never forget that floating bridge,
Now I will never forget that floating bridge,
Now I will never forget that floating bridge,
Tell me: five minutes time in the water I would be in.

Now when I was rollin' down, I would fall on my hands,
Now when I was rollin' down, I would fall on my hands,
Now when I was rollin' down, I would fall on my hands,
Please take me on dry land.

Now they carried me in the house and they laid me 'cross the bed,
Now they carried me in the house and they laid me 'cross the bed,
Now they carried me in the house and they laid me 'cross the bed,
'Bout a gallon of muddy water I have drunk.

They dried me off and they laid me in the bed,
They dried me off and they laid me in the bed,
They dried me off and they laid me in the bed,
Couldn't hear nothin' but muddy water in ma head.

And people was standing on the bridge – was screamin' and cryin',
And people was standing on the bridge – was screamin' and cryin',
And people was standing on the bridge – was screamin' and cryin',
"Lord have mercy – where we gwine*?"   [= going]

AMERICAN BLUES SONG

from THE SATIRE OF THE TRADES

I have seen the smith at work
At the opening of his furnace;
With fingers like claws of a crocodile
He stinks more than fish roe.

The jewel-maker bores with his chisel
In hard stone of all kinds;
When he has finished the inlay of the eye,
His arms are spent, he's weary;
Sitting down when the sun goes down,
His knees and back are cramped.

The barber barbers till nightfall,
He betakes himself to town,
He sets himself up in his corner,
He moves from street to street,
Looking for someone to barber.
He strains his arms to fill his belly,
Like the bee that eats as it works.

The reed-cutter travels to the Delta to get arrows;
When he has done more than his arms can do,
Mosquitoes have slain him,
Gnats have slaughtered him,
He is quite worn out.

The washerman washes on the shore
With the crocodile as neighbour;
"Father, leave the flowing water,"
Say his son, his daughter,
It is not a job that satisfies
His food is mixed with dirt,
No limb of his is clean
He is given women's clothes,
He weeps as he spends the day at his washboard
One says to him, "Soiled linen for you."

I'll speak of the fisherman also,
His is the worst of all the jobs;
He labours on the river,
Mingling with crocodiles.
When the time of reckoning comes,
He is full of lamentations;
He does not say, "There's a crocodile,"
Fear has made him blind.
Coming from the flowing water
He says, "Mighty god!"

ANCIENT EGYPTIAN POEM

ON AGEING

When you see me sitting quietly,
Like a sack left on the shelf,
Don't think I need your chattering,
I'm listening to myself.
Hold! Stop! Don't pity me!
Hold! Stop your sympathy!
Understanding if you got it,
Otherwise I'll do without it!

When my bones are stiff and aching
And my feet won't climb the stairs,
I will only ask one favour:
Don't bring me no rocking chair.

When you see me walking, stumbling,
Don't study and get it wrong.
'Cause tired don't mean lazy
And every goodbye ain't gone.
I'm the same person I was back then,
A little less hair, a little less chin,
A lot less lungs and much less wind,
But ain't I lucky I can still breathe in.

MAYA ANGELOU

13

ALL'S DONE

All's done.
All's said.
To-night
In a strange bed
Alone
I lie.
So slight
So hid
As in a chrysalid
A butterfly.

ANON.

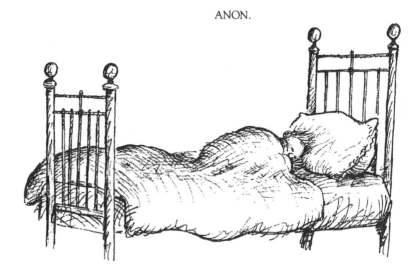

'AT SIXTY I, DIONYSIOS'

At sixty I, Dionysios of Tarsos, lie here –
not having married
and wishing my father hadn't.

ANON.
(translated from Greek by Peter Jay)

from BIRMINGHAM* JACK OF ALL TRADES

Chorus
I'm a roving Jack of all trades,
Of every trade and all trades,
And if you want to know my name,
They call me Jack of all trades.

In Aston Street I did make glass,
In Coleshill Street a baker;
In Woodcock Street I did cast brass,
In Duke Street was a Quaker.
In the Horse Fair sold crumpets rare,
Made penny wigs in Cox Street;
At Lady Well I kept a bath,
In Hurst Street I sold dogs' meat.

In Swallow Street made bellows-pipes,
In Wharf Street was a blacksmith;
In Beak Street there I did sell tripe,
In Freeman Street a locksmith.
In Cherry Street I was a quack,
In Summer Lane sold pancakes;
Oh then at last I got a knack
To manufacture worm-cakes.

In Wood Street I sold sandpaper,
In Buck Street I sold prayer books;
In Duddeston Street made pattern cards,
In Doe Street I sold fish-hooks.
In Ashted I made jew's-harp springs,
In Thomas Street made awl blades;
So now you know the ups and downs
Of a jolly Jack of all trades.

ANON.

---

* Birmingham was once known as 'the city of a thousand trades'.

BLACKSMITHS

Swarthy smoke-blackened smiths, smudged with soot,
Drive me to death with the din of their banging.
Men never knew such a noise at night!
Such clattering and clanging, such clamour of scoundrels!
Crabbed and crooked, they cry, "Coal! Coal!"
And blow with their bellows till their brains burst.
"Huff! Puff!" pants one: "Haff! Paff!" another.
They spit and they sprawl and they spin many yarns.
They grate and grind their teeth, and groan together,
Hot with the heaving of their hard hammers.
Aprons they have, of hide of the bull,
And greaves as leg-guards against glowing sparks.
Heavy hammers they have, and hit hard with them;
Sturdy strokes they strike on their steel anvils.
Lus, bus! Las, bas! they beat in turn –
Such a doleful din, may the Devil destroy it!
The smith stretches a scrap, strikes a smaller,
Twines the two together, and tinkles a treble note:
Tik, tak! Hic, hac! Tiket, taket! Tyk, tak!
Bus, lus! Bas, las! Such a life they lead,
These Dobbin-dressers: Christ doom them to misery!
There's no rest at night for the noise of their water-fizzing.

ANON.
(translated from Medieval English by Brian Stone)

THE DOCTOR

TOSS POT*:
I have travelled round Italy, Spitally, France and Spain,
All round England and back again.
I can cure the itch, the stitch, the palsy and the gout,
The plague within and the plague without.
And if there be nineteen devils in that man's skull,
I'll surely cast twenty of them out.
I've got in my pocket spectacles for blind bumble bees, crutches for lame
    ducks, pack saddles for grasshoppers and many other useful things.
No! I've got a bottle in my inside, outside, rightside, leftside waist-coat
    pocket, which my grandmother sent me from Spain three days after
    she died, that will surely bring any dead man back to life again. Why!
    I cured Sir Harry of a disease twenty yards long, and surely I can cure
    this poor man of his disorder

Kneels down and hands the wounded man a bottle.

My medicine is hens pens
peasy weasy
the juice of the beetle
the bones of the ladle
the brains of a louse
the puddings of a mouse
the bumble bee's oil
the midge's treacle
the wit of a weasel
the wool of a frog
fifteen ounces of last November's fog.
Stir that up with a grey cat's feather
and blow it into a mouse's bladder,
put three drops into your left ear
and you'll get up and sing a song.

ANON.
(adapted from various Mummers' plays by MICHAEL ROSEN)

* Contemptuous name for the 'doctor'

17

A FEMALE RIP-TAIL ROARER

You just ought to see me rigged out in my best.
My bonnet is a hornet's nest,
garnished with wolves' tails and eagles' feathers.
My gown's made of a whole bear's hide,
with the tail for a train.
I can drink from the branch without a cup,
shoot a wild goose flying,
wade the Mississippi without getting wet,
out scream a catamount*,   [= mountain lion]
and jump over my own shadow.

ANON.

FIRE DOWN BELOW

There is fire in the lower hold,
There's fire down below,
Fire in the main well,
The captain didn't know.

There is fire in the forepeek,
Fire in the main,
Fire in the windlass,
Fire in the chain.

There is fire in the foretop,
Fire down below,
Fire in the chain-plates,
The boats'ain didn't know.

18

There is fire up aloft,
There is fire down below,
Fire in the galley,
The cook he didn't know.

ANON.

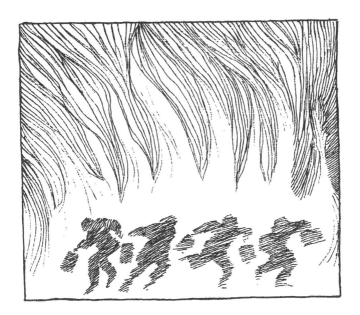

'HE WHO SPENDS MUCH'

He who spends much and gets nothing
And owes much and has nothing
And looks in his purse and finds nothing
May be sorry
So he says nothing.

ANON.
(translated from Middle English by Michael Rosen)

19

I DON'T WANT YOUR MILLIONS, MISTER

I don't want your millions, Mister,
I don't want your diamond ring,
All I want is the right to live, Mister,
Give me back my job again.

I don't want your Rolls-Royce, Mister,
I don't want your pleasure yacht,
All I want is food for my babies,
Give to me my old job back.

We worked to build this country, Mister,
While you enjoyed a life of ease,
You've stolen all that we built, Mister,
Now our children starve and freeze.

Think me dumb if you wish, Mister,
Call me green, or blue or red;
This one thing I sure know, Mister,
My hungry babies must be fed.

ANON.

I HAD A NICKEL

I had a nickel and I walked around the block.
I walked right into a baker shop.
I took two doughnuts right out of the grease;
I handed the lady my five-cent piece.
She looked at the nickel and she looked at me,
And said, "This money's no good to me.
There's a hole in the nickel, and it goes right through."
Says I, "There's a hole in the doughnut, too."

ANON.

LUBBERLAND

There is a ship we understand
Now riding in the river,
It's just come from Lubberland,
There's nowhere like it ever.
You who love a lazy life,
You ought now to go over,
Lubberland is not much more
Than two thousand miles from Dover.

The captain says, in every town
Hot roasted pigs will meet ye;
In the streets, they run up and down
Crying out, "Please come and eat me."
Hot custard pies grow on the trees,
Each ditch is full of rich jellies.
Now if you listen to me now
Go there and fill your bellies.

ANON.
(adapted from 17th Century English by MICHAEL ROSEN)

PORTENTS AND PRODIGIES*

Upon the eighteenth of this present *May*,
A tempest strange, pray mind me what I say:
So strange, I think the like was never known,
As I can hear of yet by any one.

Hail-stones as big as eggs apace down fell,
And some much bigger, as I hear some tell:
Who took them up as they lay on the ground,
And measured, they were found eight inches round.

The very fowls that flew up in the air
Were stricken dead, it plainly doth appear:
Wings from their bodies parted by this hail,
A story true, although a dreadful tale.

ANON.

*Omens and unnatural happenings.

THE REST OF THE DAY'S YOUR OWN

One day when I was out of work a job I went to seek,
To be a farmer's boy.
At last I found an easy job at half a crown a week,
To be a farmer's boy.
The farmer said, "I think I've got the very job for you;
Your duties will be light, for this is all you've got to do:
Rise at three every morn, milk the cow with the crumpled horn,
Feed the pigs, clean the sty, teach the pigeons the way to fly,
Plough the fields, mow the hay, help the cocks and hens to lay,
Sow the seeds, tend the crops, chase the flies from the turnip tops.
Clean the knives, black the shoes, scrub the kitchen and sweep the flues,
Help the wife, wash the pots, grow cabbages and carrots,
Make the beds, dust the coals, mend the gramophone,
And then if there's no more work to do, the rest of the day's your own."

I scratched my head and thought it would be absolutely prime
To be a farmer's boy.
The farmer said, "Of course you'll have to do some overtime,
When you're a farmer's boy."
Said he, "The duties that I've given you, you'll be quickly through,
So I've been thinking of a few more things that you can do:
Skim the milk, make the cheese, chop the meat for the sausagees,
Bath the kids, mend their clothes, use your dial* to scare the crows,   [= face]
In the milk, put the chalk, shave the knobs off the pickled pork,
Shoe the horse, break the coal, take the cat for his midnight stroll,
Cook the food, scrub the stairs, teach the parrot to say his prayers,
Roast the joint, bake the bread, shake the feathers up in the bed,
When the wife's got the gout, rub her funny bone,
And then if there's no more work to do, the rest of the day's your own."

I thought it was a shame to take the money, you can bet,
To be a farmer's boy.
And so I wrote my duties down in case I should forget
I was a farmer's boy.
It took all night to write 'em down, I didn't go to bed,

But somehow I got all mixed up, and this is how they read:
Rise at three, every morn, milk the hen with the crumpled horn,
Scrub the wife every day, teach the nanny goat how to lay,
Shave the cat, mend the cheese, fit the tights on the sausagees,
Bath the pigs, break the pots, boil the kids with a few carrots,
Roast the horse, dust the bread, put the cocks and hens to bed,
Boots and shoes, black with chalk, shave the hair on the pickled pork,
All the rest I forgot, somehow it had flown,
But I got the sack this morning, so that the rest of my life's my own.

ANON.

SELFISHNESS

Great spenders are bad lenders.

ANON.

SUMMER IS GONE

I have but one story –
The stags are moaning,
The sky is snowing,
Summer is gone.

Quickly the low sun
Goes drifting down
Behind the rollers,
Lifting and long.

The wild geese cry
Down the storm;
The ferns have fallen,
Russet and torn.

The wings of the birds
Are clotted with ice.
I have but one story –
Summer is gone.

ANON.
(translated from 9th Century Irish by Sean O'Faolain)

THE SURPRISING NUMBER 37

The number 37 has a special magic to it.
If you multiply 37 × 3, you get   111.
If you multiply 37 × 6, you get   222.
If you multiply 37 × 9, you get   333.
If you multiply 37 × 12, you get   444.
If you multiply 37 × 15, you get   555.
If you multiply 37 × 18, you get   666.
If you multiply 37 × 21, you get   777.
If you multiply 37 × 24, you get   888.
If you multiply 37 × 27, you get   999.

ANON.

A VERY OLD SPELL TO SAY OUT LOUD
TO GET RID OF WARTS

Wart, wart, wart-chicken
you must not start building here
you must not have a house here
you must head north from here
to the nearest hill
where, horrible thing
you have a brother.
He will put a leaf by your head.
Oh wither forever
under the foot of a wolf
under the eagle's wing
under the eagle's claw.
Die like coal in the fireplace
shrink like dung on the wall
dry up like water in a jug.
Become as small as a grain of linseed
smaller even than a skin-worm's hip-bone.
Become so small
that
you
become
nothing.

ANON.
(translated from Middle English by Michael Rosen)

A WICKED TONGUE

A wicked tongue sets England and France
Fighting each other with spear and lance.

A wicked tongue can break a bone
Though a tongue itself has none.

ANON.
(translated from Middle English by Michael Rosen)

WRITTEN 500 YEARS AGO

Bruised muscles, broken bones,
Strife, rowing and empty homes,
Lame in old age and bent double,
These are the beauties of playing football.

ANON.
(translated from Middle English by Michael Rosen)

WORRIED SONG

It takes a worried man to sing a worried song
It takes a worried man to sing a worried song
I'm worried now, but I won't be worried long;

If anybody asks you who made up this song
If anybody asks you who made up this song
Tell them it was me and I sing it all day long.

ANON.

DEEP-PILED SNOW

When the deep-piled winter snow
melted on her roof, it caved
the timbers in and killed her, but
her neighbours did not make a grave;
they left her in her friendly room,
her tomb her home, her home a tomb.

ANTIPATER OF THESSALONIKA
(translated by Robin Skelton)

27

WHILE REEDS STAND

I who say I am somebody
Tremble when the earth quakes,
Cling when the ground shakes
From the weight of the elephant.
Why should I, Tomezo,
    Tell me Tomezo,
    Why should I,
When even the ant
Continues its foraging
Along the dancing walls
To the tops of the craggy mountains,
As if nothing happens.
To that little ant and its kind
There is no trembling
Neither is there any clinging,
Yet I who say am somebody
Dodge under the inanimate* table   [= lifeless]
Shame!
    Why should I, Tomezo
    Tell me Tomezo, Oh
    Why should it be me!

SELBY ASHONG-KATAI

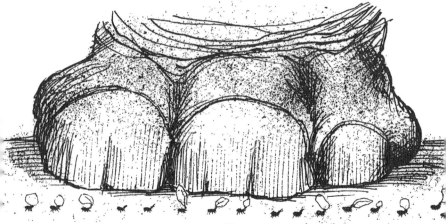

28

SONG 21

The tongue of the Lightning flashes along the top of the clouds . . .
Making them shine like red ochre*, flashing along the yellow clouds . . . [= clay]
The Lightning Snake moving its tail, rearing its head quickly from
   its hole . . .
Great Lightning Snake, flashing along on the clouds:
Coming out from its camp, striking the clouds . . .
The Snake, salt-water creature making thin streaks of lightning.
The tongue of the Lightning flashes along the top of the clouds . . .
Making them shine like red ochre, flashing along the yellow clouds . . .

AUSTRALIAN ABORIGINE POEM

from SONGS OF THE FALLEN

We mourned for ourselves, our lot.
Broken spears lie in the by-ways,
we have torn out our hair by the roots.

Palaces stood roofless, blood-red walls.
Maggots swarm the squares and huts.
Our city walls are stained with shattered brains.

Water flows red, as if someone had dyed it,
and if we drink
it tastes of sulphur.

In grief we beat our fists
against the walls of our mud houses,
a net of holes our only heritage.

Our strength was in our shields
but shields could not resist this desolation.

29

We have eaten cakes baked of linnets,
chewed dog-grass that tastes of nitre;
we have swallowed lumps of clay, lizards, rats,
farm soil turned dry dust, even maggots . . .

AZTEC
(translated by Edward Kissam and Michael Schmidt)

OTOMI POEM

The river goes by, goes by
and never stops.
The wind goes by, goes by
and never stops.

Life goes by
and never comes back.

AZTEC
(translated by Edward Kissam and Michael Schmidt)

I WAS

I was in a cartoon on television. I was a broom standing in a corner.
I swept floors with my feet. I didn't like sweeping floors.
I was bought from a store.
I was able to talk.
I was a movable broom.
I was very mad because all I did was sweep.
I was finally so mad I turned right back into a tree.
I threw my trees of oranges at the people I swept floors for.

ILONA BABURKA

SOME DAYS

Some days leave
some days grieve
some days you almost don't believe.
Some days believe you,
some days don't,
some days believe you
and you won't.
Some days worry
some days mad
some days more than make you
glad.
Some days, some days,
more than shine,
witnesses,
coming on down the line!

JAMES BALDWIN

31

HAIKU

Winter downpour –
even the monkey
needs a raincoat.

BASHO
(translated by Lucien Stryk)

THE MERE*
(from *Beowulf*)

HROTHGAR*:
I have heard it said
by my people and by my advisers
that they have seen
two huge wanderers in the waste-lands,
spirits from another world
keeping to the moor-lands.
One of them, like a woman
as far as they could tell,
the other wretched creature
like a man in shape
but bigger than any human
walking the path of an outcast.

The country people
since olden times have called him Grendel.
They know of no father for him
nor whether any other creature
like that was ever born amongst the evil spirits
Who live in a lost land of wind-blown cliffs
and dangerous marshland paths,
a place where wolves run to
where a mountain stream flows
down under dark cliffs
and floods under the ground.

Not far from here lies the Mere
over it hangs the frost-covered branches
of deep-rooted trees
Any night there you might see a frightening and
wonderful thing:
fire on water.
No wise man of woman born
knows how deep it is.
The strong-horned stag
who strides across the heath
seeks out a forest when he is hunted down by hounds
but he would sooner give up his life
rather than enter the Mere.

When the wind blows up a wicked storm
the surging waters
rise up darkly from there
to the clouds above
until the air becomes gloomy
and the skies weep.

(translated from Old English by Michael Rosen)

* A mere is a kind of lake
* The leader of the Danes

33

LISTN BIG BRODDA DREAD, NA!

My sista is younga than me.
My sista outsmart five-foot three.
My sista is own car repairer
and yu nah catch me doin judo with her.

    I sey I wohn get a complex.
    I wohn get a complex.
    Then I see the muscles my sista flex.

My sista is tops at disco dance.
My sista is well into self-reliance.
My sista plays guitar and drums
and wahn see her knock back double rums.

    I sey I wohn get a complex.
    I wohn get a complex.
    Then I see the muscles my sista flex.

My sista doesn mind smears of grease and dirt.
My sista'll reduce yu with sheer muscle hurt.
my sista says no guy goin keep her phone-bound –
with own car mi sista is a wheel-hound.

    I sey I wohn get a complex.
    I wohn get a complex.
    Then I see the muscles my sista flex.

JAMES BERRY

ARJUNA'S DESPAIR BEFORE THE BATTLE
(from *The Bhagavad Gita*˚)

ARJUNA:
Drive my chariot, Krishna˚ immortal, and place it between the two armies.

That I may see those warriors who stand there eager for battle, with whom I must now fight at the beginning of this war.

That I may see those who have come here eager and ready to fight, in their desire to do the will of the evil son of Dhrita-rashtra.

SANJAYA:
When Krishna heard the words of Arjuna he drove their glorious chariot and placed it between the two armies.

And facing Bhishma and Drona and other royal rulers he said: "See, Arjuna, the armies of the Kurus, gathered here on this field of battle."

Then Arjuna saw in both armies fathers, grandfathers, sons, grandsons; fathers of wives, uncles, masters; brothers, companions and friends.

When Arjuna thus saw his kinsmen face to face in both lines of battle, he was overcome by grief and despair and thus he spoke with a sinking heart.

ARJUNA:
When I see all my kinsmen, Krishna, who have come here on this field of battle,

Life goes from my limbs and they sink, and my mouth is sear and dry; a trembling overcomes my body, and my hair shudders in horror;

My great bow Gandiva falls from my hands, and the skin over my flesh is burning; I am no longer able to stand, because my mind is whirling and wandering.

And I see forebodings of evil, Krishna. I cannot foresee any glory if I kill my own kinsmen in the sacrifice of battle.

Because I have no wish for victory, Krishna, nor for a kingdom, nor for its pleasures. How can we want a kingdom, Govinda˚, or its pleasures or even life.

When those for whom we want a kingdom, and its pleasures, and the joys of life, are here in this field of battle about to give up their wealth and their life?

Facing us in the field of battle are teachers, fathers and sons; grandsons, grandfathers, wives' brothers; mothers' brothers and fathers of wives.

These I do not wish to slay, even if I myself am slain. Not even for the kingdom of the three worlds: how much less for a kingdom of the earth!

If we kill these evil men, evil shall fall upon us: what joy in their death could we have, O Janardana, mover of souls?

I cannot therefore kill my own kinsmen, the sons of king Dhritarashtra, the brother of my own father. What happiness could we ever enjoy, if we killed our own kinsmen in battle?

Even if they, with minds overcome by greed, see no evil in the
destruction of a family, see no sin in the treachery to friends;

Shall we not, who see the evil of destruction, shall we not refrain from
this terrible deed?

O day of darkness! What evil spirit moved our minds when for the sake
of an earthly kingdom we came to this field of battle ready to kill our
own people?

Better for me indeed if the sons of Dhrita-rashtra, with arms in hand,
found me unarmed, unresisting, and killed me in the struggle of war.

SANJAYA:
Thus spoke Arjuna in the field of battle, and letting fall his bow and
arrows he sank down in his chariot, his soul overcome by despair and
grief . . .

(translated from Sanskrit by Juan Mascaró)

* A sacred book of the Hindu religion
* Krishna is the Hindu god-prince
* Govinda is a familiar name for Krishna

CITY SIGHTS

I was looking at houses
        being knocked down
And thinking
God, look at this rubbish
And darkness!
Mess all around the street –
I feel sorry for the empty roads,
What a bad treat the streets have!
Bricks are lying idle
        in the streets

SHAZIA BI

from THE SONG OF SOLOMON

The voice of my beloved! behold, he cometh
Leaping upon the mountains, skipping upon the hills.
My beloved is like a roe or a young hart:
Behold, he standeth behind our wall,
He looketh forth at the windows,
Shewing himself through the lattice*.   [= bars]
    My beloved spake, and said unto me,
Rise up, my love, my fair one, and come away.
For, lo, the winter is past,
The rain is over and gone;
The flowers appear on the earth;
The time of the singing of birds is come,
And the voice of the turtle is heard in our land;
The fig tree putteth forth her green figs,
And the vines with the tender grape
Give a good smell.
Arise, my love, my fair one, and come away.
O my dove, that art in the clefts of the rock,
In the secret places of the stairs,
Let me see thy countenance*,   [= face]
Let me hear thy voice;
For sweet is thy voice, and thy countenance is comely.
    Take us the foxes, the little foxes, that spoil the vines:
For our vines have tender grapes.
My beloved is mine, and I am his:
He feedeth among the lilies.
Until the day break, and the shadows flee away,
Turn, my beloved, and be thou like a roe or a young hart
Upon the mountains of Bether.

THE BIBLE

38

THE SICK ROSE

O rose, thou art sick!
The invisible worm
That flies in the night,
In the howling storm,

Has found out thy bed
Of crimson joy,
And his dark secret love
Does thy life destroy.

WILLIAM BLAKE

INFANT SORROW

My mother groan'd! my father wept.
Into the dangerous world I leapt:
Helpless, naked, piping loud:
Like a fiend hid in a cloud.

Struggling in my father's hands,
Striving against my swaddling bands,
Bound and weary I thought best
To sulk upon my mother's breast.

WILLIAM BLAKE

PREPARING TO TRAVEL

In my suitcase
I pack
neither clothes nor shoes

I take
the mountain and valley
so that
nothing will happen
behind my back
Not summer nor winter

ELISABETH BORCHERS
(translated by Anneliese Wagner)

WHAT NO SNOW?

Why doesn't it snow?
It's winter, isn't it?
Then it's supposed to snow.
How else can you make snowmen,
Or fight each other with snowballs,
And slide down hills on sledges?

40

It's not fair, is it?
Soon it will be summer,
Then it'll just rain and rain for months.
Can't anyone tell me,
WHY DOESN'T IT SNOW?

BILL BOYLE

MAGNOLIA AVENUE

The name of the street was Magnolia Avenue,
but there were never any magnolias on it.
In the spring it was muddy.
Snot-nosed Dotty lived next door.
Wearing rubber boots, she waded
in the wet brown ooze, called out to me,
"Come on in, the water's fine."
There was beautiful thick mud that morning
all over my stockings.
My mother scolded, called me away inside.

I climbed the stairway from the front hallway
to slide down the banister all afternoon,
once, twice, a dozen, twenty times.
"You'll hurt yourself," my mother called, grumbling.
"You'll ruin your flowered panties."

I fell asleep playing with paper dolls.

In the evening after supper
I stood by the kitchen window eating cake
looking across at the window of Dotty's house.
Dotty's mother had black lace curtains.
They were drawn tight. Nobody looked out.

"Come away from the window," Mother said.
"Someone will think you're spying."

I never saw the inside of that room
and it was years before I saw magnolias.

ELIZABETH BREWSTER

LONDON SNOW

When men were all asleep the snow came flying,
In large white flakes falling on the city brown,
Stealthily and perpetually settling and loosely lying,
    Hushing the latest traffic of the drowsy town;
Deadening, muffling, stifling its murmurs failing;
Lazily and incessantly floating down and down;

42

Silently sifting and veiling road, roof and railing;
Hiding difference, making unevenness even,
Into angles and crevices softly drifting and sailing.
    All night it fell, and when full inches seven
It lay in the depth of its uncompacted lightness,
The clouds blew off from a high and frosty heaven;
    And all woke earlier for the unaccustomed brightness
Of the winter dawning, the strange unheavenly glare;
The eye marvelled – marvelled at the dazzling whiteness;
    The ear hearkened to the stillness of the solemn air;
No sound of wheel rumbling nor of foot falling,
And the busy morning cries came thin and spare.
    Then boys I heard, as they went to school, calling;
They gathered up the crystal manna to freeze
Their tongues with tasting, their hands with snow-balling;
    Or rioted in a drift, plunging up to the knees;
Or peering up from under the white-mossed wonder,
"O look at the trees!" they cried. "O look at the trees!"
    With lessened load, a few carts creak and blunder,
Following along the white deserted way,
A country company long dispersed asunder:
    When now already the sun, in pale display
Standing by Paul's high dome, spread forth below
His sparkling beams, and awoke the stir of the day.
    For now doors open, and war is waged with the snow;
And trains of sombre men, past tale of number,
Tread long brown paths, as toward their toil they go:
    But even for them awhile no cares encumber*   [= burden]
Their minds diverted; the daily word is unspoken,
The daily thoughts of labour and sorrow slumber
At the sight of the beauty that greets them, for the charm
    they have broken.

ROBERT BRIDGES

BOYS HUNTING A SQUIRREL

Then as a nimble squirrel from the wood,
Ranging the hedges for his filberd-food*,   [= hazel nut]
Sits pertly on a bough his brown nuts cracking,
And from the shell the sweet white kernel taking,
Till with their crooks and bags a sort of boys,
To share with him, come with so great a noise
That he is forc'd to leave a nut nigh broke,
And for his life leap to a neighbour oak,
Thence to a beech, thence to a row of ashes;
Whilst through the quagmires, and red water plashes,
The boys run dabbling through thick and thin;
One tears his hose*, another breaks his shin,   [= long socks]
This, torn and tatter'd, hath with much ado
Got by the briars; and that hath lost his shoe;
This drops his band; that headlong falls for haste;
Another cries behind for being last;
With sticks and stones and many a sounding holloa,
The little fool, with no small sport, they follow,
Whilst he, from tree to tree, from spray to spray,
Gets to the wood, and hides him in his dray.

WILLIAM BROWNE OF TAVISTOCK

from CHILD LABOUR

"For oh," say the children, "we are weary
   And we cannot run or leap;
If we cared for any meadows, it were merely
   To drop down in them and sleep.
Our knees tremble sorely in the stooping,
   We fall upon our faces, trying to go;
And underneath our heavy eyelids drooping
   The reddest flower would look as pale as snow.
For, all day, we drag our burden tiring
   Through the coal-dark, underground;
Or, all day, we drive the wheels of iron
   In the factories, round and round.

For all day the wheels are droning, turning;
   Their wind comes in our faces,
Till our hearts turn, our heads with pulses burning,
   And the walls turn in their places:
Turns the sky in the high window, blank and reeling,
   Turns the long light that drops adown the wall,
Turn the black flies that crawl along the ceiling:
   All are turning, all the day, and we with all.
And all day, the iron wheels are droning,
   And sometimes we could pray,
"O ye wheels" (breaking out in a mad moaning)
   "Stop! be silent for to-day!"

ELIZABETH BARRETT BROWNING

MEETING AT NIGHT

The grey sea and the long black land;
And the yellow half-moon large and low;
And the startled little waves that leap
In fiery ringlets from their sleep,
As I gain the cove with pushing prow,
And quench its speed i' the slushy sand.

Then a mile of warm sea-scented beach;
Three fields to cross till a farm appears;
A tap at the pane, the quick sharp scratch
And blue spurt of a lighted match,
And a voice less loud, thro' its joys and fears,
Than the two hearts beating each to each!

ROBERT BROWNING

SO WE'LL GO NO MORE A ROVING

So, we'll go no more a roving
   So late into the night,
Though the heart be still as loving,
   And the moon be still as bright.

For the sword outwears its sheath,
   And the soul wears out the breast,
And the heart must pause to breathe,
   And love itself have rest.

Though the night was made for loving,
   And the day returns too soon,
Yet we'll go no more a roving
   By the light of the moon.

LORD BYRON

THE JABBERWOCKY

'Twas brillig, and the slithy toves
   Did gyre and gimble in the wabe;
All mimsy were the borogoves,
     And the mome raths outgrabe.

"Beware the Jabberwock, my son!
   The jaws that bite, the claws that catch!
Beware the Jubjub bird, and shun
     The frumious Bandersnatch!"

He took his vorpal sword in hand:
   Long time the manxome foe he sought –
So rested he by the Tumtum tree,
     And stood awhile in thought.

And as in uffish thought he stood,
   The Jabberwock, with eyes of flame,
Came whiffling through the tulgey wood,
     And burbled as it came!

One, two! One, two! And through and through
   The vorpal blade went snicker-snack!
He left it dead, and with its head
     He went galumphing back.

"And hast thou slain the Jabberwock?
   Come to my arms, my beamish boy!
O frabjous day! Callooh! Callay!"
     He chortled in his joy.

'Twas brillig, and the slithy toves
   Did gyre and gimble in the wabe;
All mimsy were the borogoves,
     And the mome raths outgrabe.

LEWIS CARROLL

SLEEPING

He slept on his hands.
On a rock.
On his feet.
On someone else's feet.
He slept on buses, trains, in airplanes.
Slept on duty.
Slept beside the road.
Slept on a sack of apples.
He slept in a pay toilet.
In a hayloft.
In the Super Dome*.
Slept in a Jaguar, and in the back of a pickup.
Slept in theatres.
In jail.
On boats.
He slept in line shacks and, once, in a castle.
Slept in the rain.
In blistering sun he slept.
On horseback.
He slept in chairs, churches, in fancy hotels.
He slept under strange roofs all his life.
Now he sleeps under the earth.
Sleeps on and on.
Like an old king.

RAYMOND CARVER

* The Super Dome is the world's largest indoor stadium in New Orleans, USA.

MY MOTHER SAW A DANCING BEAR

My mother saw a dancing bear
By the schoolyard, a day in June.
The keeper stood with chain and bar
And whistle-pipe, and played a tune.

And bruin* lifted up its head   [= brown bear]
And lifted up its dusty feet,
And all the children laughed to see
It caper in the summer heat.

They watched as for the Queen it died.
They watched it march. They watched it halt.
They heard the keeper as he cried,
"Now, roly-poly!" "Somersault!"

50

And then, my mother said, there came
The keeper with a begging-cup,
The bear with burning coat of fur,
Shaming the laughter to a stop.

They paid a penny for the dance,
But what they saw was not the show;
Only, in bruin's aching eyes,
Far-distant forests, and the snow.

CHARLES CAUSLEY

THE WHIRLWIND IS WICKED

The whirlwind is wicked:
It pulls the grass from the thatch.
Where do poor people stay?

The whirlwind is wicked;
After cleaning the house
It puts all the rubbish back.

The whirlwind is wicked;
The thief steals what is fascinating
And finishes by throwing out the children's clothes.

The whirlwind is wicked;
It spreads the soil on the flat rock
Where people can put their washing.

The whirlwind is wicked;
It broadcasts the weeds in the gardens;
It laughs at those who are weeding.

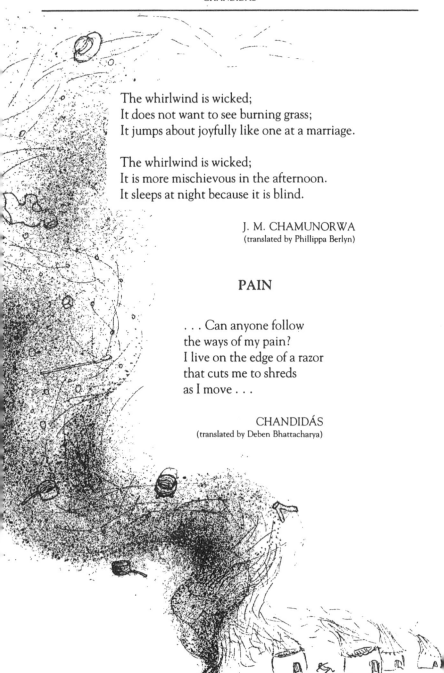

The whirlwind is wicked;
It does not want to see burning grass;
It jumps about joyfully like one at a marriage.

The whirlwind is wicked;
It is more mischievous in the afternoon.
It sleeps at night because it is blind.

J. M. CHAMUNORWA
(translated by Phillippa Berlyn)

PAIN

. . . Can anyone follow
the ways of my pain?
I live on the edge of a razor
that cuts me to shreds
as I move . . .

CHANDIDÁS
(translated by Deben Bhattacharya)

'I WANT A SANDWICH'

I
WANT
A
SANDWICH
WITH
SOME
HAM
AND
SOME
CHEESE
AND
SOME
BUTTER
AND
SOME
MUSTARD
AND
SOME
SALT
AND
SOME
PEPPER
AND
SOME
TOMATO
AND
SOME
LETTUCE
AND
SOME
MAYONNAISE
AND
SOME
KETCHUP
AND
SOME
RELISH
AND
YES
SOME
BREAD

REMY CHARLIP

THE DAY OF THE TOURNAMENT
(from *The Knight's Tale, The Canterbury Tales*)

And on the morrow, when that day gan spring,
Of horse and harness noise and clattering
There was in hostelries all about;
And to the palace rode there many a rout
Of lords upon steeds and palfreys*. [palfrey = small horse]
There might you see devising of harness
So uncouth* and so rich and wrought so well [uncouth = strangely foreign]
Of goldsmithry, of broidery and of steel;
The shields bright, testers* and trappures*, [testers = head pieces]
  [trappures = trappings]
Gold-hewn helmets, hauberks*, coat-armours; [hauberks = chain-mail]
Lords in parementz* on their coursers, [parementz = finely dressed]
  [courser = war-horse]
Knights of retinue, and eek* squires [eek = also]
Nailing the spears, and helmets buckling,
Jigging of shields and laniers* lacing [laniers = thongs]
(There, as needs be, there was no thing idle);
The foamy steeds on the golden bridle
Gnawing; and fast the armourers also

With file and hammer pricking to and fro;
Yeomen on foot, and commoners many one
With short staves, thick as they may go;
Pipes, trumpets, nackers*, clarions*,   [nackers = drums]
That in the battle blow bloody sounds;   [clarions = bugles]
The palace full of people up and down,
Here three, there ten, holding their question,
Devining of these Theban knights two,
Some said thus, some said, "It shall be so."
Some held with him with the black beard,
Some with the bald, some with the thick hair;
Some said he looked grim and he would fight;
"He has a sparth* of twenty pound of weight."
Thus was the hall full of devining,
Long after that the sun gan to spring.

GEOFFREY CHAUCER
(modernized spelling from late Middle English)

CHILDHOOD

O dear to us ever the scenes of our childhood
The green spots we played in the school where we met
The heavy old desk where we thought of the wild-wood
Where we pored o'er the sums which the master had set
I loved the old church-school, both inside and outside
I loved the dear ash trees and sycamore too
The graves where the buttercups burning gold outvied
And the spire where pelitory* dangled and grew   [= a bushy plant]

The bees i' the wall that were flying about
The thistles, the henbane and mallows all day
And crept in their holes when the sun had gone out
And the butterfly ceased on the blossoms to play
O dear is the round stone upon the green hill
The pinfold* hoof printed with oxen – and bare   [= cattle enclosure]
The old princess-feather tree growing there still
And the swallows and martins wheeling round in the air

Where the chaff whipping outwards lodges round the barn door
And the dunghill cock struts with his hens in the rear
And sings 'Cockadoodle' full twenty times o'er
And then claps his wings as he'd fly in the air
And there's the old cross with its round about steps
And the weathercock creaking quite round in the wind
And there's the old hedge with its glossy red heps*   [= rose hips]
Where the green-linnet's nest I have hurried to find –

– To be in time for the school or before the bell rung.
Here's the odd martin's nest o'er the shoemaker's door
On the shoemaker's chimney the old swallows sung
That had built and sung there in the seasons before
Then we went to seek pootys* among the old furze   [= young partridges]
On the heaths, in the meadows beside the deep lake
And return'd with torn clothes all covered wi' burrs
And oh what a row my fond mother would make

Then to play boiling kettles just by the yard door
Seeking out for short sticks and a bundle of straw
Bits of pots stand for teacups after sweeping the floor
And the children are placed under school-mistress's awe
There's one set for pussy, another for doll
And for butter and bread they'll each nibble an awe*   [= haw]
And on a great stone as a table they loll
The finest small tea-party ever you saw

The stiles we rode upon 'all a cock-horse'
The mile a minute swee*   [= swing]
On creaking gates – the stools o' moss
What happy seats had we
There's nought can compare to the days of our childhood
The mole-hills like sheep in a pen
Where the clodhopper sings like the bird in the wild wood
All forget us before we are men

JOHN CLARE

A LADY COMES TO AN INN

Three strange men came to the inn,
One was a black man pocked and thin,
One was brown with a silver knife,
And one brought with him a beautiful wife.

That lovely woman had hair as pale
As French champagne or finest ale,
That lovely woman was long and slim
As a young white birch or a maple limb.

Her face was like cream, her mouth was a rose,
What language she spoke nobody knows,
But sometimes she'd scream like a cockatoo
And swear wonderful oaths that nobody knew.

Her great silk skirts like a silver bell
Down to her little bronze slippers fell,
And her low-cut gown showed a dove on its nest
In blue tattooing across her breast.

Nobody learned the lady's name
Nor the marvellous land from which they came,
But no one in all the countryside
Has forgotten those men and that beautiful bride.

ELIZABETH J. COATSWORTH

TIME, REAL AND IMAGINARY
(AN ALLEGORY)

On the wide level of a mountain's head,
(I knew not where, but 'twas some faery place)
Their pinions*, ostrich-like, for sails outspread,   [= arms]
Two lovely children run an endless race,
      A sister and a brother!
      This far outstript the other;
    Yet ever runs she with reverted face,
    And looks and listens for the boy behind:
      For he, alas! is blind!
O'er rough and smooth with even step he passed,
And knows not whether he be first or last.

SAMUEL TAYLOR COLERIDGE

from THE TWENTIES
(Refrain 2)

We must all be very kind to Auntie Jessie,
And do everything we can to keep her bright.
If when you're in the Underground
You hear her make a funny sound
It's very rude to laugh at her outright.
You must never fill her nightdress case with beetles
Or beat up her Horlick's Malted Milk to foam,
Though her kiss is worse than death
It's unkind to hold your breath
For Charity you know begins at home.

NOËL COWARD

SHORT THOUGHT

I wish I had rings running through me like trees,
Then you'd know I wasn't lying about my age.

ELAINE CUSACK

HABITS

Habits are the things you do,
That Mother says you're "NOT to"
Yet you keep on doing them,
Because, somehow, you've GOT to.
There's biting nails . . . and sniffing . . .
And there's standing on one leg,
And leaving all the white stuff,
You find inside your egg.

There's fidgeting . . . and whistling . . .
And there's shuffling with your feet.
There's sucking your lead pencil,
And 'noising' when you eat.
There's talking with your mouth full,
And tilting up your chair,
Elbows on the table,
And messing up your hair.

There's throwing stones, and grunting,
And kicking things about,
Putting hands in pockets,
When you ought to keep them out.

There's making funny faces,
And always saying "eh" . . .
Forgetting you've a hanky,
And getting in the way.

There's lots of other things as well,
I'm *always* being told!
I don't suppose I'll ever learn,
Not even when I'm old.
Because . . . I'll tell you something,
Honest! it's quite true!
Half the things that *I* do . . .
Well! DADDY does them too!

MAB DAVIS

CONTACT (1954)

I was running
running and I looked
back over my shoulder
and bounced
off Miss Simpson
so
she
bawled me out
for not looking
where I was running
but
that wasn't as bad
as knowing
the soft springy feel
of Miss Simpson's stomach.

DIANE DAWBER

THE FUNERAL

They dressed us up in black,
Susan and Tom and me;
And, walking through the fields
All beautiful to see,
With branches high in the air
And daisy and buttercup,
We heard the lark in the clouds, –
In black dressed up.

They took us to the graves,
Susan and Tom and me,
Where the long grasses grow
And the funeral tree:
We stood and watched; and the wind
Came softly out of the sky
And blew in Susan's hair,
As I stood close by.

Back through the fields we came,
Tom and Susan and me,
And we sat in the nursery together,
And had our tea.
And, looking out of the window,
I heard the thrushes sing;
But Tom fell asleep in his chair.
He was so tired, poor thing.

WALTER DE LA MARE

MISTLETOE

Sitting under the mistletoe
(Pale-green, fairy mistletoe),
One last candle burning low,
All the sleepy dancers gone,
Just one candle burning on,
Shadows lurking everywhere:
Some one came, and kissed me there.

Tired I was; my head would go
Nodding under the mistletoe
(Pale-green, fairy mistletoe);
No footsteps came, no voice, but only,
Just as I sat there, sleep, lonely,
Stooped in the still and shadowy air
Lips unseen – and kissed me there.

WALTER DE LA MARE

'A SLASH OF BLUE'

A slash of Blue –
A sweep of Gray –
Some scarlet patches on the way,
Compose an Evening Sky –
A little purple – slipped between
Some Ruby Trousers hurried on –
A Wave of Gold –
A Bank of Day –
This just makes out the Morning Sky.

EMILY DICKINSON

THE FIRE OF LONDON
(from *Annus Mirabilis*)

Such was the rise of this prodigious⋅ fire,   [= monstrous]
  Which in mean buildings first obscurely bred,
From thence did soon to open streets aspire,
  And straight to palaces and temples spread.

In this deep quiet, from what source unknown,
  Those seeds of fire their fatal birth disclose:
And first, few scattering sparks about were blown,
  Big with the flames that to our ruin rose.

Then, in some close-pent room it crept along,
  And, smouldering as it went, in silence fed:
Till th' infant monster, with devouring strong,
  Walked boldly upright with exalted head.

At length the crackling noise and dreadful blaze,
  Called up some waking lover to the sight;
And long it was ere he the rest could raise,
  Whose heavy eye-lids yet were full of night.

The next to danger, hot pursu'd by fate,
    Half clothed, half naked, hastily retire:
And frighted mothers strike their breasts, too late,
    For helpless infants left amidst the fire.

Their cries soon waken all the dwellers near:
    Now murmuring noises rise in every street:
The more remote run stumbling with their fear,
    And, in the dark, men justle as they meet.

Now streets grow thronged and busy as by day:
    Some run for buckets to the hallowed choir:
Some cut the pipes, and some the engines play,
    And some more bold mount ladders to the fire.

In vain: for, from the East, a *Belgian* wind,
    His hostile breath through the dry rafters sent:
The flames impelled, soon left their foes behind,
    And forward, with a wanton fury went.

A key of fire ran all along the shore,
    And lightened all the river with the blaze:
The wakened tides began again to roar,
    And wondering fish in shining waters gaze.

The fire, meantime, walks in a broader gross,
    To either hand his wings he opens wide:
He wades the streets, and straight he reaches cross,
    And plays his longing flames on th' other side.

At first they warm, then scorch, and then they take:
    Now with long necks from side to side they feed:
At length, grown strong, their mother fire forsake,
    And a new colony of flames succeed.

To every nobler portion of the town,
    The curling billows roll their restless tide:
In parties now they straggle up and down,
    As armies, unopposed, for prey divide.

Now day appears, and with the day the King,
 Whose early care had robbed him of his rest:
Far off the cracks of falling houses ring,
 And shrieks of subjects pierce his tender breast.

No help avails: for, *Hydra**-like, the fire,
 Lifts up his hundred heads to aim his way.
And scarce the wealthy can one half retire,
 Before he rushes in to share the prey.

Those who have homes, when home they do repair
 To a last lodging call their wandering friends.
Their short uneasy sleeps are broke with care,
 To look how near their own destruction tends.

Those who have none sit round where once it was,
 And with full eyes each wonted room require:
Haunting the yet warm ashes of the place,
 As murdered men walk where they did expire.

The most, in fields, like herded beasts lie down;
 To dews obnoxious on the grassy floor:
And while their babes in sleep their sorrows drown,
 Sad parents watch the remnants of their store.

JOHN DRYDEN

*Hydra was a many-headed monster in Greek mythology.

COMING HOME ON MY OWN THINKING

Coming Home on my own Thinking
Couldn't Wait to get home Thinking
Buzzing of the planes engines Thinking
Couldn't wait to meet me friends Thinking

I'll miss this cold country Thinking
Coming home Guyana Thinking
Back to the nice warm weather Thinking.

BRENDA DUNDAS

'WHEN THE INDIANS'

When the Indians
Sold
New York
For a handsome
Sum of
Glass beads,
They scouted west
And crossed
What is now called
The Mississippi,
Travelling west
On what is now called
Route 66
Until they arrived at
What is now called
California.
They decided to
Sell this too
For what is now
Called money,
But the whites
Took it with
What is now called
Guns.

WILLIAM EASTLAKE

BETTER BE KIND TO THEM NOW

A squirrel is digging up the bulbs
In half the time Dad took to bury them.

A small dog is playing football
With a mob of boys. He beats them all,
Scoring goals at both ends.
A kangaroo would kick the boys as well.

Birds are so smart they can drink milk
Without removing the bottle-top.

Cats stay clean, and never have to be
Carried screaming to the bathroom.
They don't get their heads stuck in railings,
They negotiate first with their whiskers.

The gecko walks on the ceiling, and
The cheetah can outrun the Royal Scot.
The lion cures his wounds by licking them,
And the guppy has fifty babies at a go.

The cicada plays the fiddle for hours on end,
And a man-size flea could jump over St Paul's.

If ever these beasts should get together
Then we are done for, children.
I don't much fancy myself as a python's pet,
But it might come to that!

D. J. ENRIGHT

FRED

Fred likes creatures
And has a lot of 'em.
Bees don't sting him,
He's got a pot of 'em,
Little round velvety bodies they are
Making honey in Fred's jam-jar.

Fred likes creatures,
Hedgehogs don't prickle him,
They flatten their quills
And scarcely tickle him,
But lie with their pointed snouts on his palm,
And their beady eyes are perfectly calm.

Fred likes creatures,
The nestling fallen out
Of the tree-top
With magpie callin' out
Where? Where? Where? contented lingers
In the round nest of Fred's thick fingers.

Fred likes creatures
Nothing's queer to him,
Ferrets, tortoises,
Newts are dear to him.
The lost wild rabbit comes to his hand
As to a burrow in friendly land.

Fred *eats* rabbit
Like any glutton, too
Fred eats chicken
And beef and mutton too.
Moral? None. No more to be said.
Than Fred likes creatures, and creatures like Fred.

ELEANOR FARJEON

THE LONDON OWL

When in our London gardens
    The brown owl hoots at night,
Smutty walls and chimney-stacks
    All seem put to flight;

That blackness past the window-pane,
    Might hold anything –
Anything wild and natural
    That moves the earth towards Spring,

Anything strange and simple,
   Any untrampled wood,
Or any broken timbered barn,
   Where once warm cattle stood,

Any dark or reedy marsh
   Out there when the brown owl calls –
Anything but the chimney-stacks
   And smutty London walls.

ELEANOR FARJEON

ORANGE

You must learn how to peel, man.
The fruit in your hand is ripe.
   Cut, so! Reel, as you ring it round,
            like a ball.
Hold the rind to your nose, man.
Smell, 'til your eyes burn. Then
Bite. And when the juice sweets your tongue,
Man,
   Let the seed fall.

BARBARA FERLAND

WRESTLING

I like wrestling with Herbie because
he's my best friend.
We poke each other
(but not very hard)
and punch each other
(but not very hard)
and roll on the grass
and pretend to have fights

just to make our sisters scream.
But sometimes if he hits me too much
and it hurts,
I get mad
and I punch him back
as hard as I can
and then we both are crying
and going into our houses
and slamming our back doors on each other.
But the next day, if it's sunny,
we come out into our yards
and grin at each other,
and sometimes he gives me an apple
or I give him a cookie and
then we start wrestling again.

KATHLEEN FRASER

71

GRAVEYARD

ROBERT FROMAN

NEITHER OUT FAR NOR IN DEEP

The people along the sand
All turn and look one way.
They turn their back on the land.
They look at the sea all day.

As long as it takes to pass
A ship keeps raising its hull;
The wetter ground like glass
Reflects a standing gull.

The land may vary more;
But whatever the truth may be –
The water comes ashore,
And the people look at the sea.

They cannot look out far.
They cannot look in deep.
But when was that ever a bar
To any watch they keep?

ROBERT FROST

HORRIBLE THINGS

"What's the horriblest thing you've seen?"
Said Nell to Jean.

"Some grey-coloured, trodden-on plasticine;
On a plate, a left-over cold baked bean;
A cloak-room ticket numbered thirteen;
A slice of meat without any lean;
The smile of a spiteful fairy-tale queen;
A thing in the sea like a brown submarine;
A cheese fur-coated in brilliant green;

73

A bluebottle perched on a piece of sardine.
What's the horriblest thing *you've* seen?"
Said Jean to Nell.

"Your face, as you tell
Of all the horriblest things you've seen."

ROY FULLER

LAY NOT UP

The bees
Sneeze and wheeze
   Scraping pollen and honey
From the lime trees:

The ants
Hurries and pants
   Storing up everything
They wants:

But the flies
Is wise
   When the cold weather comes
They dies.

L.W.G.

from MY HEART SOARS

I see my white brothers
going about blotting out nature from his cities.
I see him strip the hills bare, leaving ugly wounds
on the face of mountains. I see him tearing things
from the bosom of mother earth as though she
were a monster, who refused to share her treasures
with him. I see him throw poison in the waters,
indifferent to the life he kills there;
and he chokes the air with deadly fumes.

CHIEF DAN GEORGE

TRIPS

eeeveryyee time
when i take my bath
and comb my hair (i mean
mommy brushes it till i almost cry)
and put on my clean clothes
and they all say MY
HOW NICE YOU LOOK
and i smile and say
"thank you mommy cleaned
me up"
then i sit down and mommy says
GET UP FROM THERE YOU GONNA BE DIRTY
'FORE I HAVE A CHANCE TO GET DRESSED
MYSELF
and i want to tell her if you was
my size the dirt would catch
you up faster too

NIKKI GIOVANNI

THE VILLAGE SCHOOLMASTER
from *The Deserted Village*

Beside yon straggling fence that skirts the way,
With blossomed furze unprofitably gay,
There, in his noisy mansion, skilled to rule,
The village master taught his little school;
A man severe he was, and stern to view,
I knew him well, and every truant knew;
Well had the boding tremblers learned to trace
The day's disasters in his morning face;
Full well they laughed with counterfeited glee,
At all his jokes, for many a joke had he;
Full well the busy whisper circling round,
Conveyed the dismal tidings when he frowned;
Yet he was kind, or if severe in aught*,   [= anything]
The love he bore to learning was in fault;
The village all declared how much he knew;
'Twas certain he could write, and cypher* too;   [= do arithmetic]
Lands he could measure, terms and tides presage*,   [= predict]
And even the story ran that he could gauge.
In arguing too, the parson owned his skill,
For e'en tho' vanquished, he could argue still;
While words of learned length, and thundering sound,
Amazed the gazing rustics ranged around,
And still they gazed, and still the wonder grew,
That one small head could carry all he knew.

OLIVER GOLDSMITH

DALEY'S DORG WATTLE

"You can talk about yer sheep dorgs," said the man from Allan's Creek,
"But I know a dorg that simply knocked 'em bandy!
Do whatever you would show him, and you'd hardly need to speak;
Owned by Daley, drover cove in Jackandandy.

"We was talkin' in the parlour, me and Daley, quiet like,
When a blowfly starts a-buzzin' round the ceilin',
Up gets Daley, and he says to me, 'You wait a minute, Mike,
And I'll show you what a dorg he is at heelin'.'

"And an empty pickle-bottle was a-standin' on the shelf,
Daley takes it down and puts it on the table,
And he bets me drinks that blinded dorg would do it by himself –
And I didn't think as how as he was able!

"Well, he shows the dorg the bottle, and he points up to the fly,
And he shuts the door, and says to him – 'Now Wattle!'
And in less than fifteen seconds, spare me days, it ain't a lie,
That there dorg had got that inseck in the bottle."

N. T. GOODGE

VIDA AND ANT

Mr Vida
sat
crosslegged
beneath the cotton tree
eating fruit.

Ant laughed –
"Watch me eat
the juice
from his face
and give him a nip."

Ant crept up

Vida moved
Ant smiled
Vida squirmed
and ate
Vida wiped
Ant bit
Vida danced
Ant escaped
The cotton tree
smiled
Vida sat
and ate
and scratched
and stretched.

JEAN GOULBOURNE

TEACHING PRACTICE

Thwack! "Go on, get out of here, and don't come back!
. . . I treat them all like that, that's all they understand –
And they respect you for it, mark my words
In forty years I've never had a rowdy class – not once!

Forget that nonsense that they teach you in your
Education Course. Those lecturers don't know the score,
The simple fact that most kids just aren't human beings at all,
They're animals. They don't respond to kindness, trust –

A whip and chair is more their mark. You've got to scare
The little brutes. Yes, scare them rigid, make them live
In fear of you. That's discipline . . .

Hey – You! . . . Did you see that? The little beast was spying,
Listening to every word I've said. Go on – yes, run!
Quick! . . . Bring him back. – See me tomorrow morning, after play. –
That's how it's done! You're learning fast –
   you'll be all right."

MICK GOWAR

from AN ELEGY WRITTEN IN A COUNTRY CHURCHYARD

The *curfew*• tolls the knell of parting day,   [= evening bell]
The lowing herd winds slowly o'er the lea,
The plowman homeward plods his weary way,
And leaves the world to darkness, and to me.
   Now fades the glimmering landscape on the sight,
And all the air a solemn stillness holds;
Save where the beetle wheels his droning flight,
And drowsy tinklings lull the distant folds.

79

Save that from yonder ivy-mantled tower
The moping owl does to the moon complain
Of such as, wand'ring near her secret bower,
Molest her ancient solitary reign.

Beneath those rugged elms, that yew-tree's shade,
Where heaves the turf in many a mouldering heap,
Each in his narrow cell for ever laid,
The rude forefathers of the hamlet sleep.

The breezy call of incense-breathing morn,
The swallow twitt'ring from the straw-built shed,
The cock's shrill clarion*, or the echoing horn,   [= loud call]
No more shall rouse them from their lowly bed.

For them no more the blazing hearth shall burn,
Or busy housewife ply her evening care:
No children run to lisp their sire's return,
Or climb his knees the envied kiss to share.

Oft did the harvest to their sickle yield,
Their furrow oft the stubborn glebe* has broke;   [= soil]
How jocund* did they drive their team afield!   [= merrily]
How bowed the woods beneath their sturdy stroke!

Let no ambition mock their useful toil,
Their homely joys and destiny obscure;
Nor grandeur hear with a disdainful smile,
The short and simple Annals* of the poor.   [= records]

The boast of heraldry, the pomp of power,
And all that beauty, all that wealth e'er gave,
Awaits alike th' inevitable hour.
The Paths of Glory lead but to the grave.

THOMAS GRAY

'SUNDAY MORNING'

Sunday morning.
Me and Mama
off to church.
Smile pretty now.
Wear your nice dress,
we're going to visit the Lord's House,
she says,
then bangs her toe
and cusses.
I want to ask,
Instead of going to the Lord's house,
why don't we invite Him to visit ours?

NIKKI GRIMES

THE PEOPLE IN POVERTY

I came to a place
where they dump
all the garbage of the town.

And I saw some children
filling a few old sacks
with rusty tins
worn-out shoes
bits of old cardboard boxes.

And some flies crept in among the sacks
and then came out
and settled on the children's heads.

GLORIA GUEVARA
(translated by Peter Wright)

LAUGHING BACKWARDS

The first thing I ever knew was funny
was Sylvester Keach who walked backwards.
Sixty or so, pudgy, bald, six feet tall, who
walked backwards along the shoulder smiling at
the cars, walked backwards from his mother's place
way out on Cox Mill Road down to Ninth and Main,
then turned around and walked backwards home.

Sometimes we'd drive up to Sylvester
in Paul's Packard and honk or throw a cherry
bomb nearby, and he'd laugh and wave and keep on
walking, picking his way backwards
to town or backwards back to home.

Laugh? We laughed until we couldn't spit or speak,
and once, Paul drove us along beside
old Sylvester, driving in reverse and us all sitting
backwards in our seats. And Sylvester Keach
laughed so hard, laughed and laughed
he nearly lurched into a shrub.

You expect things like this to turn out sad,
and to look back and say, Gawd
we were little monsters to treat poor Sylvester
so pitifully, and thank the Lord we know better now.

But the joke is, Sylvester Keach walked backwards
right up till he died at 86, and his last afternoon
he'd walked backwards into town and waved at every
honking teenager and smelled the sweet gun powder
grit of cherry bombs, and laughed his hearty laugh
that anybody'd be happy to laugh on their last day.

And you'd like to think all the funeral cars drove
backwards, and they lowered him upside down
into his hole and stood around laughing,
and then drove backwards home, slinging cherry bombs
at all those tragic fools picking their way forward.

JIM HALL

A SHEEP FAIR

The day arrives of the autumn fair,
  And torrents fall,
Though sheep in throngs are gathered there,
  Ten thousand all,
Sodden, with hurdles round them reared:
And, lot by lot, the pens are cleared,
And the auctioneer wrings out his beard,
And wipes his book, bedrenched and smeared,
And rakes the rain from his face with the edge of his hand,
  As torrents fall.

The wool of the ewes is like a sponge
  With the daylong rain:
Jammed tight, to turn, or lie, or lunge,
  They strive in vain.
Their horns are soft as finger-nails,
Their shepherds reek against the rails,
The tied dogs soak with tucked-in tails,
The buyers' hat-brims fill like pails,
Which spill small cascades when they shift their stand
  In the daylong rain.

THOMAS HARDY

FLYNN OF VIRGINIA

Didn't know Flynn –
  Flynn of Virginia –
  Long as he's been 'yar?
  Look 'ee here, stranger,
Whar hev you been?

Here in this tunnel
He was my pardner,
That same Tom Flynn –
  Working together,
  In wind and weather,
Day out and in.

Didn't know Flynn!
  Well, that is queer.
Why, it's a sin
To think of Tom Flynn –
  Tom, with his cheer,
  Tom, without fear –
Stranger, look 'yar!

Thar in the drift,
  Back to the wall,
He held the timbers
  Ready to fall;
Then in the darkness
  I heard him call:

"Run for your life, Jake!
Run for your wife's sake!
Don't wait for me."
And that was all
  Heard in the din,
  Heard of Tom Flynn –
Flynn of Virginia.

BRET HARTE

I COME AND STAND AT EVERY DOOR

I come and stand at ev'ry door,
But none can hear my silent tread,
I knock and yet remain unseen,
For I am dead, for I am dead.

I'm only seven, although I died
In Hiroshima* long ago,
I'm seven now as I was then –
When children die, they do not grow.

My hair was scorched by swirling flame,
My eyes grew dim and then grew blind;
Death came and turned my bones to dust,
And that was scattered by the wind.

I need no fruit, I need no rice,
I need no sweets or even bread;
I ask for nothing for myself,
For I am dead, for I am dead.

All that I ask is that for peace,
You fight today, you fight today,
So that the children of the world
May live and grow and laugh and play.

NAZIM HIKMET

* On 6 August 1945 the first atomic bomb was exploded on Hiroshima, Japan.

MRS O'NEILL
(A Tale of Unrequited Love)

Every evening
Before she went to bed
Mrs O'Neill said
Goodnight
To that nice announcer
On her small T.V.
Because she was eighty
And very much alone

And when she died
He never even went
To her funeral

RICHARD HILL

WRITTEN ON RETURN HOME

A youngster when I left, and now
grown old I return; still with
my country dialect, but with hair
thinning; none of the children
know me, and they laughingly ask,
"Traveller, where do you come from?"

HO CHIH-CHANG
(translated by Rewi Alley)

THE HAMMERS

Noise of hammers once I heard
Many hammers, busy hammers,
Beating, shaping night and day,
Shaping, beating dust and clay
To a palace; saw it reared;
Saw the hammers laid away.

And I listened, and I heard
Hammers beating, night and day,
In the palace newly reared,
Beating it to dust and clay:
Other hammers, muffled hammers,
Silent hammers of decay.

RALPH HODGSON

SUPERMARKET

I'm
lost
among a
maze of cans
behind a pyramid
of jams, quite near
asparagus and rice,
close to the Oriental spice,
and just before sardines.
I hear my mother calling, "Joe.
Where are you, Joe?
Where did you
Go?" And I reply in a voice concealed among
the candied orange peel, and packs of Chocolate
Dreams.

88

"I
hear
you, Mother
dear, I'm here –
quite near the ginger ale
and beer, and lost among a

maze
of cans
behind a
pyramid of jams
quite near asparagus
and rice, close to the
Oriental spice, and just before sardines."

But
still
my mother
calls me, "Joe!
Where are you, Joe?
Where did you go?"

"Somewhere
around asparagus
that's in a sort of
broken glass,
beside a kind of m-

ess-
y jell
that's near a tower of cans that

f
e
l
l

and squashed the Chocolate Dreams."

FELICE HOLMAN

CLOWNS

Where do clowns go,
what do clowns eat,
where do clowns sleep,

what do clowns do,
when nobody,
just nobody laughs
any more,
Mummy?

MIROSLAV HOLUB

A QUADRUPEDREMIAN SONG

He dreamt that he saw the Buffalant,
    And the spottified Dromedaraffe,
The blue Camelotamus, lean and gaunt,
    And the wild Tigeroceros calf.

The maned Liodillo loudly roared,
    And the Peccarbok whistled its whine,
The Chinchayak leapt on the dewy sward,
    As it hunted the pale Baboopine.

He dreamt that he met the Crocoghau,
    As it swam in the Stagnolent Lake;
But everything that in dreams he saw
    Came of eating too freely of cake.

THOMAS HOOD THE YOUNGER

'REPEAT THAT, REPEAT'

Repeat that, repeat,
Cuckoo, bird, and open ear wells, heart-springs, delightfully sweet,
With a ballad, with a ballad, a rebound
Off trundled timber and scoops of the hillside ground, hollow
hollow hollow ground
The whole landscape flushes on a sudden at a sound.

GERARD MANLEY HOPKINS

GROWING UP
(Concluded?)

He ran
 hard
  down the misty
  alley
   to catch up
    the footsteps
     round the corner

     but when he
     got there he
    heard them
   die away
  nothing
 but echoes
of
   his
       own –

MICHAEL HOROVITZ

MOVING IN

Moving out
Of an old crowd
trying
to move
Into a new crowd
But no one
wants to know
you
At all.

But when
you make them
feel stupid
And make them
look small
Everybody
wants to be your friend
Everybody
wants to be your friend
Everyone around
you
You seem to know.

MARISA HORSFORD

CROSS

My old man's a white old man
And my old mother's black.
If ever I cursed my white old man
I take my curses back.

If ever I cursed my black old mother
And wished she were in hell,
I'm sorry for that evil wish
And now I wish her well.

My old man died in a fine big house.
My ma died in a shack.
I wonder where I'm gonna die,
Being neither white nor black?

LANGSTON HUGHES

HOPE

Sometimes when I'm lonely,
Don't know why,
Keep thinkin' I won't be lonely
By and by.

LANGSTON HUGHES

FLORIDA ROAD WORKERS

I'm makin' a road
For the cars
To fly by on.
Makin' a road
Through the palmetto* thicket   [= palm tree]

For light and civilization
To travel on.

Makin' a road
For the rich old white men
To sweep over in their big cars
And leave me standin' here.

Sure,
A road helps all of us!
White folks ride –
And I get to see 'em ride.
I ain't never seen nobody
Ride so fine before.
Hey buddy!
Look at me.
I'm making a road!

LANGSTON HUGHES

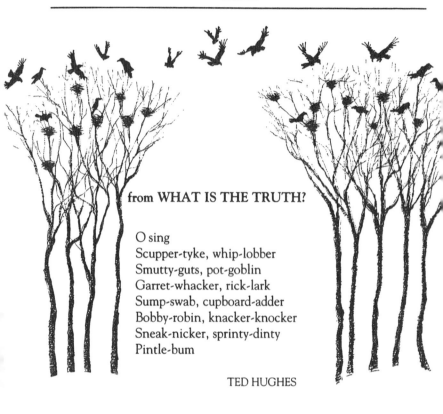

from WHAT IS THE TRUTH?

O sing
Scupper-tyke, whip-lobber
Smutty-guts, pot-goblin
Garret-whacker, rick-lark
Sump-swab, cupboard-adder
Bobby-robin, knacker-knocker
Sneak-nicker, sprinty-dinty
Pintle-bum

TED HUGHES

THE STAG

While the rain fell on the November woodland shoulder of Exmoor
While the traffic jam along the road honked and shouted
Because the farmers were parking wherever they could
And scrambling to the bank-top to stare through the tree-fringe
Which was leafless,
The stag ran through his private forest.

While the rain drummed on the roofs of the parked cars
And the kids inside cried and daubed their chocolate and fought
And mothers and aunts and grandmothers

Were a tangle of undoing sandwiches and screwed-round gossiping
    heads
Steaming up the windows,
The stag loped through his favourite valley.

While the blue horsemen down in the boggy meadow
Sodden nearly black, on sodden horses,
Spaced as at a military parade,
Moved a few paces to the right and a few to the left and felt rather
    foolish
Looking at the brown impassable river,
The stag came over the last hill of Exmoor.

While everybody high-kneed it to the bank-top all along the road
Where steady men in oilskins were stationed at binoculars,
And the horsemen by the river galloped anxiously this way and that
And the cry of hounds came tumbling invisibly with their echoes down
    through the draggle of trees,
Swinging across the wall of dark woodland,
The stag dropped into a strange country.

And turned at the river
Hearing the hound-pack smash the undergrowth, hearing the bell-note
Of the voice that carried all the others,
Then while his limbs all cried different directions to his lungs, which
    only wanted to rest,
The blue horsemen on the bank opposite
Pulled aside the camouflage of their terrible planet.

And the stag doubled back weeping and looking for home up a valley
    and down a valley
While the strange trees struck at him and the brambles lashed him,
And the strange earth came galloping after him carrying the loll-
    tongued hounds to fling all over him
And his heart became just a club beating his ribs and his own hooves
    shouted with hounds' voices,
And the crowd on the road got back into their cars
Wet-through and disappointed.

TED HUGHES

97

from PROFESSOR BRANESTAWM'S DICTIONARY

Aaron	What a wig has.
abandon	What a hat has.
abundance	A waltz for cakes.
accord	A piece of thick string.
addition	What a dinner table has.
aftermath	The next lesson after arithmetic.
already	Completely crimson.
boycott	Bed for a male baby.
buoyant	Male insect.
copper nitrate	What policemen get paid for working overtime in the evenings.
cross purposes	Bad-tempered fish.
dozen	Opposite of what one does.
during	Did you use the bell?
enchant	A female chicken's song.
fungi	A comedian.
furlong	The coat of a Persian cat.
hyacinth	Familiar greeting for Cynthia.
jargon	The vase is no longer here.

khaki	A thing for starting a motor car.
knapsack	Sleeping bag.
liability	Capacity for telling untruths.

macadam	The first Scotsman.

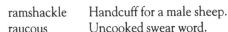

offal	Terrible.
out of bounds	A frog too tired to leap.
oxide	Leather.
pasteurize	Across your vision.

ramshackle	Handcuff for a male sheep.
raucous	Uncooked swear word.
rheumatic	An apartment at the top of a house.
robust	A line of knitting that has come undone.
sediment	What he announced he had in mind.
shamble	Imitation male cow.

statue	Enquiry as to whether it is yourself.
urchin	The lower part of the lady's face.
versatile	Poetry on the roof.
vertigo	In which direction did he proceed?
Windsor	Did you succeed at your game, guv'nor?

NORMAN HUNTER

THE BIG FIB
from *Peer Gynt*

PEER GYNT:
While I sheltered from the weather,
hidden by a clump of bushes,
a buck was scraping at the snow-crust
after moss –
I stood listening, hardly breathing,
– heard the scraping of his hoof-tip –
till I saw one branching antler;
then I carefully crept forward
on my belly through the stones,
till around a boulder's cover
I could peep . . . You've never seen
such a buck! So sleek and fat!
Then I fired!
Down the buck crashed on the hillside,
but the instant that he stumbled
I was straddled on his shoulders
with his left ear in my grasp,
just about to plunge my knife in
where the backbone joins the skull.
Hey! The ugly creature bellowed –
leaping to his feet at once!
As he rose, the sudden lurching
jerked my sheath-knife out of my hand;
but his antlers held my legs pinned,
tightly gripped against his loins,
holding me as in a vice.
Then, with a sudden leap, he bounded
right along the ridge of Gjendin!
Have you ever
seen that mountain ridge at Gjendin?
All of half a mile it stretches,
sheer and sharp as the blade of a scythe.
Either side, if you look downwards,
over glacier, scar, and hillside,
you can see, across the ash-grey

scree, deep into brooding waters
dark as if asleep – and more than
thirteen hundred yards below!

All the ridge's length, we two
cut our way against the wind.
Such a colt I never rode!

There in the mid-air straight before us
seemed to hang the blazing sun.
Halfway down towards the waters
tawny backs of eagles hovered
through the wide and dizzy void,
till they swung like specks behind us.

On the shores below, the ice-floes
crashed and splintered, yet no murmur
reached us, only swirling mist-shapes
leapt like dancers, weaving – singing –
round about our eyes and ears.

101

Suddenly up a cock-grouse rocketed
from the rocks where he'd been crouching –
flapping, cackling, terrified –
right beneath the buck's foot, balanced
sheer above a break-neck cliff.

With a start as high as heaven,
turning half about, the reindeer
plunged us both down to the depths!
At our backs, the gloomy rock-face –
under us, the deep abyss!

First we hurtled through a cloud-sheet,
next we split a flock of sea-gulls
scattering them in all directions
while they filled the air with screeching.

Downwards without pause we hurtled;
till below us something glistened
whitish, like a reindeer's belly . . .
Mother, it was our reflection
shooting from the glassy water
with the self-same crazy motion
as ours, rushing down to meet it.
Buck from the air and buck from the surface
clashed their horns in a single moment,
so that the foam splashed all about us.

There we were, then, in the water!
He swam, I hung on behind him,
till at long, long last we struggled
somehow to the northern shore . . .
I came home –

MOTHER:
Yes, but the buck, Peer?

PEER GYNT:
Oh, he's probably still there!
If you find him, you can have him!

HENRIK IBSEN
(translated by Peter Watts)

SONG OF A HUMAN WOMAN

I married him.
and we lived on.

Every day
he would go into the mountains
and would bring home
bear
and deer.
I lived in plenty,
lacking nothing
that I wished to eat,
and lacking nothing
that I desired to have.

Then one day
from the heavens
a cuckoo with a beautiful voice,
a cuckoo which sang very skilfully
came down
and lighted atop the spirit fence.
Raising its tail,
bobbing its tail
in this direction
and in that direction,
that cuckoo
sang on and on
both night
and day.

My wedded husband
remained
with his face turned away
before
the food which was tasty
and the food which was not tasty.

103

I would cook
and serve the food
to my wedded husband,
but he
remained
without eating anything.
The foods I had served him first
were covered
with black mould,
and the foods I had served him later
were covered
with white mould.
Day after day,
for six full days,
and night after night,
for six full nights
the cuckoo sang on.
Then the sound of the cuckoo ceased.

One day
my wedded husband
got up.
The ashes at the edges of the fireplace
he raked out towards the centre,
and the ashes in the centre of the fireplace
he raked out towards the edges.
Here and there
he traced furrows and lines.
As he did this,
he spoke these words:

"My wedded wife,
listen well
to what I have to say!
I am not
a human at all
whom you have married.
Who I am is this:

"In the heavens
are six brothers,
Thunder Gods,
and the youngest of them
am I.
When I looked
among the gods,
there was not a single one
who was to my liking.
When I looked
among the humans,
you alone
were to my liking
on account of your disposition,
your skill at needlework,
and your beauty.
For this reason
I came down
in secret
and married you.
My elder brothers
have now found me,
and the lord of the cuckoos
was sent down
from the heavens
to harangue me.
You probably
thought that this
was nothing but
an ordinary cuckoo
singing,
but the lord of the cuckoos
was saying that
if I do not return home
I will be banished
to the Country-without-birds,
to the Land-without-birds.
By all means
I must return home.

"Even though I return home,
I bid you not to weep.
Make for yourself
silken hoods,
sixfold hoods.
Each year
wear one of them
and discard them one by one.
In the meantime
there will be gods travelling overhead.
First of all
a quiet rumbling
will come along.
At the very last
will come thunder
with a crunching, crashing rumbling.
When there comes a god
thundering like that,
it will be me.

"Since I am a god indignant
at being separated from his wife,

I will be
the god who thunders
with a crunching, crashing rumbling.
Go outside,
and make as if
you are doing something or other.
If you do this,
you yourself
will not be able to see me,
but I, being a god,
will be able to see you.
This is what you must do
from now on.

"One more thing –
after you have worn
and discarded
all six of the hoods,
you will marry
another young man
who will be like me.
Rather than

Stirring with a wooden spoon,
I finished cooking
the goodly cereal.
Stacking
delicate bowls
on a delicate tray,
I served the meal
to my wedded husband.
Receiving it,
he ate several mouthfuls
as if to taste the flavour;
then the remainder of the bowl
he proffered to me.
Receiving it,
I lifted it up high
and lowered it down low,
and ate the food.

Though I had thought
that it would happen later,
my wedded husband
stood up.
I clung to both hems
of his robe.
Crying out
"My dear husband!"
I screamed out
loud and long,
clinging to both hems
of his robe.
My wedded husband
seemed to make
a flapping motion.
Then he turned
into a bird larger
than any bird
and flew out through the window.
I caught a glimpse
of him sitting

your marrying me,
who am a god,
it will be better
for both of you
to be humans
married to each other.

"Now I want to eat
of your goodly cooking.
Cook food quickly!"

At these words of his,
I hung over the fire
a pretty little pot.
Into the pot
I poured with a splash
the treasured grains.

atop the spirit fence.
I went outside
and threw myself down
on the sandy beach.
As I continued
to weep,
that bird
raised its tail
and bobbed its tail
in this direction
and in that direction
and the teardrops it shed
rained down
like a summer cloudburst.

That bird
went flying up
and circled over me,
the teardrops it shed
raining down
like a summer cloudburst.
It swooped down
and grazed me with its wings,
then it flew up again
and withdrew
into the skies.
Though it seemed to me
that it had gone far off yonder,
six more times
it flew back towards me,
circled over me,
and grazed me with its wings,
the teardrops it shed
raining down
like a summer cloudburst.
After that
it ascended toward the skies
and withdrew
into the highest heavens.

"What was it
my wedded husband
said?"
I thought to myself.

Weeping,
I went back
into the house.
Then I made for myself
silken hoods,
sixfold hoods,
and wore one of them.

As time went on,
when thunder would come rumbling,
first of all

a quiet rumbling
would come along.
At the very last
there would come thunder
with a crunching, crashing rumbling.
Knowing that
this was the sound
of my divine husband coming,
I would go outside
and would make as if
I were doing something or other.
I myself
would not be able
to see
my divine husband,
but I thought that
he could see me,
and I lived on
with this

as my only pleasure.
When I had discarded
all six hoods,
one day
a young man
came, and
I married him.

Every day
he would go into the mountains
and would bring home
bear
and deer.
I lived in plenty,
lacking nothing
that I wished to eat,
and lacking nothing
that I desired to have,
but I never

s able to like
 human husband,
 d I was unable
 forget
 divine husband
 en for a single day.

 time went on,
 ildren were born to us,
 th boys
 d girls.
 it
 ways
 enever thunder would come rumbling,
 ould go outside
 d would make as if
 ere doing something or other.
 ould think that
 y divine husband
 uld see me,

and I lived on
with this
as my only pleasure.

As for the children,
the boys
have grown up,
and they go with their father
to do different kinds of hunting.
And the girls
who are older
help me.
They help me to gather
different food plants.

Now I am old and heavy of foot,
and as my death approaches,
I tell the story of it
to you, my children:
about how, long ago,
when I was young
the youngest one
of the six brothers,
Thunder Gods,
came down
in secret
to marry me.
I married him,
and we lived on together
until his elder brothers
found him out,
and he returned home,
a god indignant
at being separated from his wife,
a god whose thunder
has a crunching, crashing rumbling.

JAPANESE AINU
(translated by Donald L. Philippi)

109

FOUR LITTLE TIGERS

Four little tigers
   Sitting in a tree;
One became a lady's coat –
   Now there's only three.

Three little tigers
   Neath a sky of blue:
One became a rich man's rug –
   Now there's only two.

Two little tigers
   Sleeping in the sun:
One a hunter's trophy made –
   Now there's only one.

One little tiger
   Waiting to be had:
Oops! He got the hunter first –
   Aren't you kind of glad?

FRANK JACOBS

WASP IN A ROOM

Chase me, follow me round the room, knock over
Chairs and tables, bruise knees, spill books. High
I am then. If you climb up to me I go
Down. I have ways of detecting your least
Movements. I have radar you did not
Invent. You are afraid of me, I can
Sting hard. Ah but watch me bask in
The, to you, unbearable sun. I sport with it, am
Its jester and also its herald. Fetch a

Fly whisk. I scorn such. You must invent stings
For yourselves or else leave alone, small, flying,
Buzzing tiger who have made a jungle out of the room
    you thought safe,
Secure from all hurts and prying.

ELIZABETH JENNINGS

RAINBOW

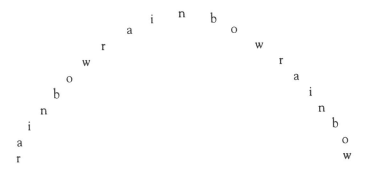

JILL

MY HAIR-CUT

I do not need your mirror
My barber is my brother.

A. W. KAYPER-MENSAH

111

THE DOORMAN

The doorman dreams of the door.
His hat is blue, braided
with hotel gold.
Today he opened the door
sometimes one way,
sometimes the other
with a smile apparent under
his moustache.
The double doors split before the guests
who sailed out or lapped home.
He moved before or behind
his grave moustache turning upwards
like a black November leaf.
He enlarged the door space fully
to give passage to the rapid guests.
In bed, to sleep, he counts
up the reversing swish.
One pull inwards, one pull outwards,
two inwards, two outwards
till he ebbs on a hoovered carpet
printed with whirlpools,
then flows to, on steel pivots
and sleeps and snores.

In the dream, his
shoulders are solid ice,
his hat wheels around lightly,
his teeth are huge glass panels
inside
that swing to, and grind
and swing back.

JUDITH KAZANTZIS

THE PESSIMIST

Nothing to do but work,
   Nothing to eat but food,
Nothing to wear but clothes,
   To keep one from going nude.

Nothing to breathe but air,
   Quick as a flash 'tis gone;
Nowhere to fall but off,
   Nowhere to stand but on.

Nothing to comb but hair,
   Nowhere to sleep but in bed,
Nothing to weep but tears,
   Nothing to bury but dead.

Nothing to sing but songs,
   Ah, well, alas! alack!
Nowhere to go but out,
   Nowhere to come but back.

Nothing to see but sights,
   Nothing to quench but thirst,
Nothing to have but what we've got.
   Thus through life we are cursed.

Nothing to strike but a gait;
   Everything moves that goes.
Nothing at all but common sense
   Can ever withstand these woes.

B. J. KING

WATER

Send it cascading over waterfalls,
And break it with a roaring crash across rocks.
Wash in it, cool with it, drink it, heat with it,
Keep fish in it, kill people by the sheer force of it.
Put out fires with it, rust metal with it,
Swim in it, wade in it, dive in it, splash in it, open your eyes in it,
Journey across to France on it,
Freeze it and break glass as it expands,
Heat it and put it in radiators to warm the body,
Or just make cement and build with it.
Let it pour from the sky in tiny droplets,
And leave it as dew to make the daffodils sparkle in spring.
Let it flow in rivers, make electricity from it,
Run it along the gutters, washing the stone, and sail boats on it.
Water flowers with it, wash cars with it, make fountains of it,
But most of all
Just leave it shimmering in a river or pool
And watch, but watch carefully or it will go,
And never return.

JONATHAN KINGSMAN

SONG OF THE GALLEY-SLAVES

We pulled for you when the wind was against us and the sails were low.
  Will you never let us go?
We ate bread and onions when you took towns, or ran aboard quickly
  when you were beaten back by the foe.
The captains walked up and down the deck in fair weather singing
  songs, but we were below.
We fainted with our chins on the oars and you did not see that they
  were idle, for we still swung to and fro.
  Will you never let us go?

The salt made our oar-handles like shark-skin; our knees were cut to the bone with salt-cracks; our hair was stuck to our foreheads; and our lips were cut to the gums, and you whipped us because we could not row.

Will you never let go?

But, in a little time, we shall run out of the port-holes as the water runs along the oar-blade, and though you tell the others to row after us you will never catch us till you catch the oar-thresh and tie up the winds in the belly of the sail. Aho!

Will you never let us go?

RUDYARD KIPLING

THE COKE

I stand staring,
as Gary raises the bottle,
wishing he will ask me if I want a drink.
A pleading expression forms on my face,
but no words leave his mouth.
Two pursed lips open.
"Ah . . ." he sighs.
The bottle drops,
and he wipes from above his mouth
a coke moustache.

BRIAN KIRK

'WHEN I WAS TWENTY-ONE'

When I was twenty-one
all the other boys marched
off to war and died
while I stayed at home
with my clubfoot.

I understood the meaning
of this thirty years later
when I was walking
in the forest
with my young nephew.

We came to a cleared area
where a twisted tree
stood alone and alive
in a graveyard
of short stumps.

My nephew pointed to the tree:
"Look how useless that tree is"
and I answered
"Look how old that tree is"
without thinking.

WILLIAM J. KLEBECK

THANK-YOU LETTER

Dear Aunty Grace, ~~Mum said I had to~~
I'm writing this letter just to say
~~I hate that terrible dress you sent~~
I adore the dress you sent today.

~~Erk! Mauve!~~ The colour's just terrific!
Those little puff sleeves are really neat!
Frilly socks to match! It's just too much!
~~I'd rather wear blisters on my feet!~~

Mum says the dress looks sweetly charming.
It suits me now I'm growing up.
~~When I was made to try that thing on~~
~~I totally felt like throwing up!~~

The lace around the hem's ~~a nightmare~~
~~I won't wear that ghastly dress!~~ a dream!
I've never seen such pretty ruffles.
~~I hope I wake up before I scream!~~

You shouldn't have spent so much money,
but thanks for such a lovely surprise –
~~of all the dum dum birthday presents,~~
~~yours, Aunty Grace, easily takes first prize!~~

You're very generous. With some luck
~~I can lose the socks.~~ So thanks again
~~ink spilled on mauve I hope won't wash out~~
for the wonderful dress! Love from Jane
x x

ROBIN KLEIN

117

'I AM THE MAIDEN'

I am the maiden in bronze set over the tomb of Midas *.
As long as water runs from wellsprings, and tall trees burgeon *,   [= bud]
and the sun goes up the sky to shine, and the moon is brilliant,
as long as rivers shall flow and the wash of the sea's breakers,
so long remaining in my place on this tomb where the tears fall
I shall tell those who pass that Midas lies here buried.

KLEOBOULOS
(translated by Richmond Lattimore)

* A Greek king whose touch turned all to gold.

'NEVER SAW IT'

never saw it
never heard it
never smelt it, touched it, tasted it
never felt it
never heard it mentioned
never had any idea of it
never dreamt of it
never wanted it
never missed it
never lost it
never found it

R. D. LAING

'WHY DID THE PEACOCK SCREAM?'

Why did the peacock scream?
    in order to hear himself

why did the peacock scream?
    because he couldn't see himself

R. D. LAING

118

THE GEORGES

George the First was always reckoned
Vile, but viler George the Second;
And what mortal ever heard
Any good of George the Third?
When from earth the Fourth descended
(God be praised!) the Georges ended.

WALTER SAVAGE LANDOR

PHILOSOPHY

Two men look out through the same bars;
One sees mud – and one sees stars.

FREDERICK LANGBRIDGE

POVERTY

from *A Vision Concerning Piers Plowman*

The neediest are our neighbours if we give heed to them,
Prisoners in the dungeon, the poor in the cottage,
Charged with a crew of children and with a landlord's rent.
What they win by their spinning to make their porridge with,
Milk and meal, to satisfy the babes,
The babes that continually cry out for food,
This they must spend on the rent of their houses,
Ay, and themselves suffer with hunger,
With woe in winter rising a-nights,
In the narrow room to rock the cradle,
Carding, combing, clouting, washing, rubbing, winding,
    peeling rushes.
Pitiful it is to read the cottage-woman's woe,
Ay and many another that puts a good face on it,
Ashamed to beg, ashamed to let the neighbour know
All that they need, noontide and evening.
Many the children and nought but a man's hands
To clothe and feed them; and few pennies come in.
And many mouths to eat the pennies up.
Bread and thin ale for them are a banquet,
Cold flesh and cold fish are like roast venison,
A farthing's worth of mussels, a farthing's worth of cockles,
Were a feast to them on Fridays or fast-days.
It were a charity to help these that be at heavy charges,
To comfort the cottager, the crooked and the blind.

ABOUT WHEN YOU GET HOME

Your mum says, "Get that bedroom tidied up",
Your dad says, "Get that bike of yours put away",
And if you have got a brother he bosses you about,
And when you go to bed he keeps talking in the night,
And if you are in the same bed he pulls all the quilt away,
And if he reads books and they are heavy,
When he has finished looking at them
He drops them on you in the night.

WILLIAM LAPWORTH

SELF-PITY

I never saw a wild thing
sorry for itself.
A small bird will drop frozen dead from a bough
without ever having felt sorry for itself.

D. H. LAWRENCE

WHATEVER MAN MAKES

Whatever man makes and makes it live
lives because of the life put into it.
A yard of India muslin is alive with Hindu life.
And a Navajo woman, weaving her rug in the pattern of her dream
must run the pattern out in a little break at the end
so that her soul can come out, back to her.

But in the odd pattern, like snake-marks on the sand
it leaves its trail.

D. H. LAWRENCE

THE DONG WITH A LUMINOUS NOSE

When awful darkness and silence reign
Over the great Gromboolian plain,
Through the long, long wintry nights;
When the angry breakers roar
As they beat on the rocky shore;
When Storm-clouds brood on the towering heights
Of the Hills of the Chankly Bore:
Then, through the vast and gloomy dark,
There moves what seems a fiery spark,
A lonely spark with silvery rays
Piercing the coal-black night,
A meteor strange and bright:
Hither and thither the vision strays,
A single lurid light.

Slowly it wanders, pauses, creeps,
Anon it sparkles, flashes and leaps;
And ever as onward it gleaming goes
A light on the Bong-tree stems it throws.
And those who watch at that midnight hour
From Hall or Terrace, or lofty Tower,
Cry, as the wild light passes along,
"The Dong! – the Dong!
The wandering Dong through the forest goes!
The Dong! – the Dong!
The Dong with a luminous Nose!"

Long years ago
The Dong was happy and gay,
Till he fell in love with a Jumbly Girl
Who came to those shores one day.
For the Jumblies came in a Sieve, they did,
Landing at eve near the Zemmery Fidd
Where the Oblong Oysters grow,
And the rocks are smooth and grey.
And all the woods and the valleys rang
With the Chorus they daily and nightly sang,
"Far and few, far and few,
Are the lands where the Jumblies live;
Their heads are green, and their hands are blue,
And they went to sea in a sieve."

Happily, happily passed those days!
While the cheerful Jumblies staid;
They danced in circlets all night long,
To the plaintive pipe of the lively Dong,
In moonlight, shine, or shade.
For day and night he was always there
By the side of the Jumbly Girl so fair,
With her sky-blue hands, and her sea-green hair.
Till the morning came of that hateful day
When the Jumblies sailed in their sieve away,
And the Dong was left on the cruel shore
Gazing, gazing for evermore,

Ever keeping his weary eyes on
That pea-green sail on the far horizon,
Singing the Jumbly Chorus still
As he sate all day on the grassy hill,
"Far and few, far and few,
Are the lands where the Jumblies live;
Their heads are green, and their hands are blue,
And they went to sea in a sieve. "

But when the sun was low in the West
The Dong arose and said,
"What little sense I once possessed
Has quite gone out of my head!"
And since that day he wanders still
By lake and forest, marsh and hill,
Singing – "O somewhere, in valley or plain
Might I find my Jumbly Girl again!
For ever I'll seek by lake and shore
Till I find my Jumbly Girl once more!"
Playing a pipe with silvery squeaks,
Since then his Jumbly Girl he seeks,
And because by night he could not see,
He gathered the bark of the Twangum Tree
On the flowery plain that grows.
And he wove him a wondrous Nose,
A Nose as strange as a Nose could be!
Of vast proportions and painted red,
And tied with cords to the back of his head.
In a hollow rounded space it ended
With a luminous lamp within suspended,
All fenced about
With a bandage stout
To prevent the wind from blowing it out;
And with holes all round to send the light,
In gleaming rays on the dismal night.

And now each night, and all night long,
Over those plains still roams the Dong;

124

And above the wail of the Chimp and Snipe
You may hear the squeak of his plaintive pipe
While ever he seeks, but seeks in vain
To meet with his Jumbly Girl again;
Lonely and wild, all night he goes,
The Dong with a luminous Nose!
And all who watch at the midnight hour,
From Hall or Terrace, or lofty Tower,
Cry, as they trace the Meteor bright,
Moving along through the dreary night,
"This is the hour when forth he goes,
The Dong with a luminous Nose!
Yonder – over the plain he goes;
He goes!
He goes;
The Dong with a luminous Nose!"

EDWARD LEAR

ROBBER J. BADGUY

Robber J. Badguy
Was robbing a bank,
His manners were mean
And his underwear stank.

The neighbours got angry
As grizzly bears,
Bumped him and thumped him
And threw him downstairs.

DENNIS LEE

BLACKBIRD

Blackbird singing in the dead of night
Take these broken wings and learn to fly.
All your life
You were only waiting for this moment to arise.
Blackbird singing in the dead of night
Take these sunken eyes and learn to see.
All your life
You were only waiting for this moment to be free.
Blackbird fly, Blackbird fly
Into the light of the dark black night.
Blackbird fly, Blackbird fly
Into the light of the dark black night.
Blackbird singing in the dead of night
Take these broken wings and learn to fly.
All your life
You were only waiting for this moment to arise
You were only waiting for this moment to arise
You were only waiting for this moment to arise

JOHN LENNON
PAUL McCARTNEY

HEROINE

On Dec. 1, 1955
Mrs Rosa Parks, a 42-year-old Negro seamstress,
was ordered by a Montgomery City Lines bus driver
to get up and make way for
some white passengers.
She refused,
was arrested
and fined $10.

> *Time* – January 16, 1956
> (found by JULIUS LESTER)

TOUCH
from *Prison Notes*

When I get out
I'm going to ask someone
   to touch me
   very gently please
   and slowly,
   touch me
   I want
   to learn again
   how life feels.

I've not been touched
for seven years
   for seven years
   I've been untouched
   out of touch
   and I've learnt
   to know now
   the meaning of
   untouchable.

Untouched – not quite
I can count the things
that have touched me

One: fists
At the beginning
　　fierce mad fists
　　beating beating
　　till I remember
　　screaming
　　Don't touch me
　　please don't touch me.

Two: paws
The first four years of paws
　　every day
　　patting paws, searching
　　– arms up, shoes off
　　legs apart –
　　prodding paws, systematic
　　heavy, indifferent
　　probing away
　　all privacy.

I don't want fists and paws
I want
　　to be touched
　　again
　　and to touch,
　　I want to feel alive
　　again
　　I want to say
　　when I get out
Here I am
please touch me.

HUGH LEWIN

PEARLS

Dad gave me a string of pearls for my birthday.
They aren't real pearls but they look real.
They came nested in deep, deep blue velvet
   in a hinged box with a silvery lid.
His sister had some like them when she was my age.
She was thrilled.
He thought I'd really like them.
I said I did.

I love the box.

JEAN LITTLE

BESSIE BY DAY

This here
dirt just
gotta go,

Bessie frown
and Bessie know.
Put a
kerchief
on her head,

Beat that dirt
until it dead.

That much
better,
Bessie say

as she smile
and walk away.

MYRA COHN LIVINGSTON

129

NEVER EVER TELL

He always had a good excuse
To stay away from games.
On the hottest days
He would stay fully-clothed.
He never came swimming.

I remember
One day our class –
Called to the medical room –
Asked to strip to the waist.
He pretended not to hear
His name called
Again and again.
With tears in his eyes,
He pulled his jumper over his head
And fumbled his buttons.
He stopped,
Walked over to the nurse
Whispered in her ear.
She pointed to the screens,
He stepped behind them and waited his turn.
When it came
He rushed from behind to the Doctor's office
Hoping none of us would see.

But we did.
And we couldn't understand
The fuss.
Lots of people have eczema.

MICHAEL LOWE

130

THE FISHERMAN'S WIFE

When I am alone,
The wind in the pine-trees
Is like the shuffling of waves
Upon the wooden sides of a boat.

AMY LOWELL

A LONDON THOROUGHFARE TWO A.M.

They have watered the street,
It shines in the glare of lamps,
Cold, white lamps,
And lies
Like a slow-moving river,
Barred with silver and black.
Cabs go down it,
One,
And then another.
Between them I hear the shuffling of feet,
Tramps doze on the window-ledges,
Night walkers pass along the sidewalks.
The city is squalid and sinister,
With the silver-barred street in the midst,
Slow-moving,
A river leading nowhere.

Opposite my window,
The moon cuts,
Clear and round,
Through the plum-coloured night
She cannot light the city;
It is too bright.
It has white lamps,
And glitters coldly.

I stand in the window and watch the moon.
She is thin and lusterless,
But I love her.
I know the moon,
And this is an alien city.

AMY LOWELL

'MEAN OLD HERMON'

Mean old Hermon
dreamt he'd spent
all his money
and hanged himself
for fear of
dreaming it again.

LUCILIUS
(translated by Peter Porter)

A COUNTRY MAN COMES TO LONDON

Into London I began to walk,
It's the best town in all the land;
[= pea-pods]   "Hot peas-cods•", someone calls,
"Strawberry ripe", and "Cherry on the branch".
One bid me come near and buy some spice
"Pepper and saffron", they began to say,
"Cloves, corn, and flowers of rice",
    but I had no money with me that day.

Then I went forth by London Stone
All along Old Cannon Street;
Some drapers called to me just then,
"Loads of cheap cloth", they did shout,

but up comes one and cries, "Hot sheep's feet!"
"Rushes fair and green", another calls out;
Both cod and mackerel there I meet
   but I had no money with me that day.

Then I walked down to Eastcheap
One cried, "Ribs of beef!" and "Many a pie",
Pewter pots, they clattered in a heap
There were harps and pipes and a psaltery
"By God, yes," "By God, no," the people cry
Some sing "Jenkin" or "Julian" to get some pay
I would love to have stayed for the minstrelsy˙   [= singing]
   but I had no money with me that day.

JOHN LYDGATE
(translated from 14th Century English by Michael Rosen)

A SWAMP ROMP

Clomp Thump
Swamp Lump
Plodding in the Ooze,
Belly Shiver
Jelly Quiver
Squelching in my shoes.

Clomp Thump
Romp Jump
Mulching all the Mud,
Boot Trudge
Foot Sludge
Thud! Thud! Thud!

DOUG MACLEOD

'THE SHY SPEECHLESS SOUND'

The shy speechless sound
of a fruit falling from its tree,
and around it the silent music
of the forest, unbroken . . .

OSIP MANDELSTAM
(translated by Clarence Brown)

WINDIGO

Hair like burnt moose moss
Head like a meat ball
Eyes like burning red ashes
Nose like a pig nose
Mouth like a flaming red hoop
Lips like red circles
Voice like an angry moose call
Breath like the dump
Teeth like sharpened swords
Ears like potatoes
Neck like a bear's neck
Body like a giant
Heart like all iceberg
Arms like stretchy telephone wires
Hands like bears' claws
Legs like ice tunnels
Feet like wieners*   [= German sausages]
Toes like sliced apples

SYLVIA MARK

135

UP ON THE DOWNS

Up on the downs the red-eyed kestrels hover,
Eyeing the grass.
The field-mouse flits like a shadow into cover
As their shadows pass.

Men are burning the gorse on the down's shoulder;
A drift of smoke
Glitters with fire and hangs, and the skies smoulder,
And the lungs choke.

Once the tribe did thus on the downs, on these downs burning
Men in the frame,
Crying to the gods of the downs till their brains were turning
And the gods came.

And today on the downs, in the wind, the hawks, the grasses,
In blood and air,
Something passes me and cries as it passes,
On the chalk downland bare.

JOHN MASEFIELD

"BUTCH" WELDY

After I got religion and steadied down
They gave me a job in the canning works,
And every morning I had to fill
The tank in the yard with gasoline,
That fed the blow-fires in the sheds
To heat the soldering irons.
And I mounted a rickety ladder to do it,
Carrying buckets full of the stuff.
One morning, as I stood there pouring,
The air grew still and seemed to heave,
And I shot up as the tank exploded,
And down I came with both legs broken,
And my eyes burned crisp as a couple of eggs.
For someone left a blow-fire going,
And something sucked the flame in the tank.
The Circuit Judge said whoever did it
Was a fellow-servant of mine, and so
Old Rhodes' son didn't have to pay me.
And I sat on the witness stand as blind
As Jack the Fiddler, saying over and over,
"I didn't know him at all."

EDGAR LEE MASTERS

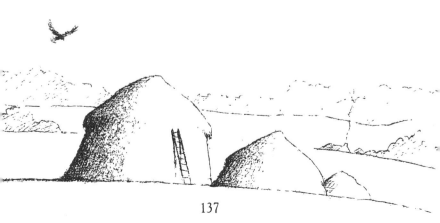

529 1983

Absentmindedly,
sometimes,
I lift the receiver
And dial my own number.

(What revelations,
I think then,
If only
I could get through to myself.)

GERDA MAYER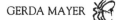

PETS

Pets are a godsend to people who enjoy the company of
small animals. Cats, for example, are very popular.
As are dogs. We had a dog once called Rover, but he
died. So now we don't call him anything.

ROGER McGOUGH

U.S. FLIES IN HAMBURGERS*

If you go down the High Street today
You'll be sure of a big surprise.
When you order your favourite burger
With a milkshake and regular fries.

For the secret is out
I tell you no lies
They've stopped using beef
In favour of FLIES

FLIES, FLIES, big juicy FLIES,
FLIES as American as apple pies.

Horseflies, from Texas, as big as your thumb
Are sautéed with onions and served in a bun.

Free-range bluebottles, carefully rinsed
Are smothered in garlic, and painlessly minced.

Black-eyed bees with stings intact
Add a zesty zing, and that's a fact.

Colorado beetles, ants from Kentucky,
Rhode Island roaches, and if you're unlucky

Baltimore bedbugs (and even horrider)
Leeches as squashy as peaches from Florida.

FLIES, FLIES, big juicy FLIES,
FLIES as American as mom's apple pies.

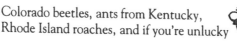
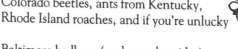
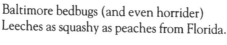

It's lovely down in MacDingles today
But if you don't fancy flies
Better I'd say to keep well away
Stay home and eat Birds' Eyes.

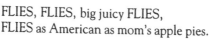
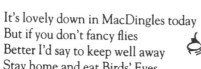
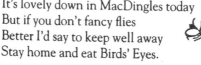

ROGER McGOUGH

Newspaper headline referring to hamburgers being airlifted to U.S. marines.

TEEF! TEEF!

Teef! Teef!
I've lost my teef!
Hash anyone sheen my teef?
You won't be able to help, I shuppose
But shomebody stole them from
under my nose!
Hash anyone sheen my teef?

COLIN McNAUGHTON

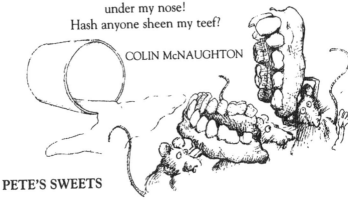

PETE'S SWEETS

Pete
will eat
anything
if it's sweet.

Peppermint soup,
or ice cream on toast.

Though what he likes most
is a jelly sandwich
without any bread.

Or instead,
a bubble-gum chop.
Chew your meat thoroughly, Pete.
"I am. Cancha hear me?" Pop!

EVE MERRIAM

SEA LOVE

Tide be runnin' the great world over:
    'Twas only last June month I mind that we
Was thinkin' the toss and the call in the breast of the lover
    So everlastin' as the sea.

Here's the same little fishes that sputter and swim,
    Wi' the moon's old glim on the grey, wet sand;
An' him no more to me nor me to him
    Than the wind goin' over my hand.

CHARLOTTE MEW

UNROLLED

At birth, experts scrutinise us
for signs of deformity.
Don't they know
our mothers always make us
just a little asymetrical
for luck, like a persian rug.

CLARE MIDGLEY

GOLIATH

They chop down 100 ft trees
To make chairs
I bought one
I am six foot one inch.
When I sit in the chair
I'm four foot two.
Did they really chop down a 100 ft tree
To make me look shorter?

SPIKE MILLIGAN

RICE PUDDING

What is the matter with Mary Jane?
She's crying with all her might and main,
And she won't eat her dinner – rice pudding again –
What *is* the matter with Mary Jane?

What is the matter with Mary Jane?
I've promised her dolls and a daisy-chain,
And a book about animals – all in vain –
What *is* the matter with Mary Jane?

What is the matter with Mary Jane?
She's perfectly well, and she hasn't a pain;
But, look at her, now she's beginning again! –
What *is* the matter with Mary Jane?

What is the matter with Mary Jane?
I've promised her sweets and a ride in the train,
And I've begged her to stop for a bit and explain –
What *is* the matter with Mary Jane?

What is the matter with Mary Jane?
She's perfectly well and she hasn't a pain,
And it's lovely rice pudding for dinner again! –
What *is* the matter with Mary Jane?

A. A. MILNE

EVE TO ADAM
(from *Paradise Lost*)

With thee conversing I forget all time,
All seasons, and their change; all please alike.
Sweet is the breath of morn, her rising sweet,
With charm of earliest birds; pleasant the sun
When first on this delightful land he spreads
His orient* beams, on herb, tree, fruit and flower,   [= from the east]
Glistering with dew; fragrant the fertile earth
After soft showers; and sweet the coming-on
Of grateful evening mild, then silent night
With this her solemn bird and this fair moon,
And these the gems of Heaven, her starry train:
But neither breath of morn when she ascends
With charm of earliest birds, nor rising sun
On this delightful land, nor herb, fruit, flower,
Glistering with dew, nor fragrance after showers,
Nor grateful evening mild, nor silent night
With this her solemn bird, nor walk by moon,
Or glittering star-light, without thee is sweet.

JOHN MILTON

143

BEBE BELINDA AND CARL COLUMBUS

VERSES FOR LAURA

There was a girl who threw bananas about
When she couldn't get bananas she threw baseball bats about
When she couldn't get baseball bats she threw big blue beehives about
And her name was Bebe, Bebe Belinda

There was a boy who threw cuckoo clocks about
When he couldn't find cuckoo clocks he threw cucumbers about
When he couldn't find cucumbers he went crackers and threw
christening cakes about
And his name was Carl, Carl Columbus

In Hanover Terrace, that magical place,
Bebe and Carl met, face to red face.
She bust his cuckoo clock with a bunch of bananas.
In a swashbuckling sword fight his cucumber cutlass
Carved her baseball bat to bits.
She bashed him on the bonce with her best blue beehive
But he craftily crowned her with a christening cake.

And they left it to me, old Lizzie Lush
To clean up the street with my scrubbing brush.

ADRIAN MITCHELL

THE TRAVEL BUREAU

All day she sits behind a bright brass rail
   Planning proud journeyings in terms that bring
   Far places near; high-coloured words that sing,
"The Taj Mahal at Agra," "Kashmir's Vale",
Spanning wide spaces with her clear detail,
   "Sevilla or Fiesole in spring,
   Through the fiords in June". Her words take wing.
She is the minstrel of the great out-trail.

At half-past five she puts her maps away,
   Pins on a grey, meek hat, and braves the sleet.
A timid eye on traffic. Dully grey
   The house that harbours her in a grey street,
   The close, sequestered, colourless retreat
Where she was born, where she will always stay.

RUTH COMFORT MITCHELL

145

FREEDOM*

When I am old I would like to have
a wife and two children
a boy and a girl and a big house
and two dogs and freedom
my friends and I would like to meet together

MOAGI

* Written by a South African child.

THE OCEAN IN LONDON

In London while I slowly wake
At morning I'm amazed to hear
The ocean, seventy miles away,
Below my window roaring, near.

When first I know that heavy sound
I keep my eyelids closely down,
And sniff the brine, and hold all thought
Reined back outside the walls of town.

So I can hardly well believe
That those tremendous billows are
Of iron and steel and wood and glass:
Van, lorry, and gigantic car.

HAROLD MONRO

from THE EARTHLY PARADISE

Folk say, a wizard to a northern king
At Christmas-tide such wondrous things did show,
That through one window men beheld the spring,
And through another saw the summer glow,
And through a third the fruited vines a-row
While still, unheard, but in its wonted way,
Piped the drear wind of that December day.

WILLIAM MORRIS

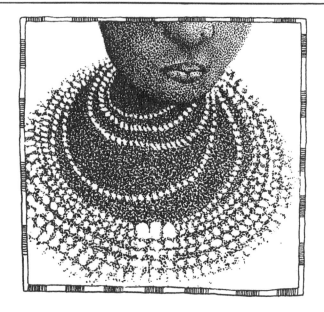

FROM POEM TO HER DAUGHTER

Daughter, take this amulet
tie it with cord and caring
I'll make you a chain of coral and pearl
to glow on your neck. I'll dress you nobly.
A gold clasp too – fine, without flaw
to keep with you always.
When you bathe, sprinkle perfume, and weave your hair in braids.
String jasmine for the counterpane.
Wear your clothes like a bride,
for your feet anklets, bracelets for your arms . . .
Don't forget rosewater,
don't forget henna for the palms of your hands.

MWANA KUPONA MSHAM

NIGHT-TIME

My Mum shouting at my brother
He's going to get hit
And sent to bed
And he won't be allowed out for a week.

When she gets cross with my brother
She shouts at me
And I get hit.

The cats are in the middle of the road.
I'm frightened a car is going to come along
And knock them down.

There's these two dogs downstairs,
One white, one black,
And whenever anyone walks past
They bite them.

When I think of all them things
It's nearly morning,
And I have to get up
And go to school.

NANCY

GRANDPA IS ASHAMED

A child need not be very clever
To learn that "Later, dear" means "Never".

OGDEN NASH

THE PEOPLE UPSTAIRS

The people upstairs all practise ballet.
Their living room is a bowling alley.
Their bedroom is full of conducted tours.
Their radio is louder than yours.
They celebrate weekends all the week.
When they take a shower, your ceilings leak.
They try to get their parties to mix
By supplying their guests with Pogo sticks,
And when their orgy at last abates,
They go to the bathroom on roller skates.
I might love the people upstairs wondrous
If instead of above us, they just lived under us.

OGDEN NASH

TOAST

I remember my Dad he was the best Dad
anyone could have
When my sister and I were young
We had such fun.
When my Mum went out for a drink,
which she did most nights,
My Dad would get out the bread
and toast it on the fire for us.
We thought this was a great treat,
with cheese on top
We would sit and he would tell us stories
of when he was a lad.
I have tasted toast which other people have made
But it wasn't as good as my Dad's.

MAUREEN NATT

SPIDER

Spider, spider
you and your wife
me and my wife
our hands you pinch, pinch
our hands you bite, bite.

NEW GUINEA POEM

THE PEANUT SELLER

Peanuts!
Two bags for five!

They brush your teeth,
They curl your hair;
They make you feel
Like a millionaire!

Peanuts!
Two bags for five!

NEW ORLEANS' STREET-CRY

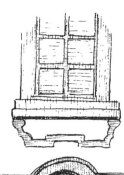

THE LITTLE CITY SQUARE

A knight-errant
With an iron gauntlet
Knocks on the door
Of the Little City Square palaces
No one opens to him
He's got the wrong door
He's got the wrong century
The last tavern is closing
He recognizes the voice of the clock
Its deep sound
He is hungry
He should be at home
Somewhere indoors

His bed is probably untouched
He's had a drop too much
Like the watchman
Who does not answer
Once more he knocks
At the wall
And falls asleep
Propped up against the façade*   [= front of a building]
Along which I am walking home
As drowsy as that iron man

VITĔZSLAV NEZVAL
(translated by Ewald Osers)

from THE WISHING BONE CYCLE
(*A North American Swampy Cree Indian Dream Poem*)

One night I was wishing things all over.
Then, I thought there were too many stars
in the sky
and not enough light down under,
in the earth.
That's when I wished a star down
for that mole
to carry on his nose.
He took it down under.
He walked around with it under there
and tried it out.
Now he comes up sometimes
to let his star talk to the other stars
in the sky.
It's dark down there
but his nose sees where he's going.
One time I wanted two moons
in the sky.
But I needed someone to look up and see
those two moons

because I wanted to hear him
try and convince the others in the village
of what he saw.
I knew it would be funny.
So, I did it.
I wished another moon up!
There it was, across the sky from the old moon.
Along came a man.
Of course I wished him down that open path.
He looked up in the sky.
He had to see that other moon!
One moon for each of his eyes!
He stood looking
up in the sky
a long time.
Then he suspected me, I think.
He looked into the trees
where he thought I might be.
But he could not see me
since I was disguised as the whole night itself!
Sometimes

154

I wish myself into looking like the whole day,
but this time
I was dressed like the whole night.
Then he said,
"There is something strange
in the sky tonight."
He said it out loud.
I heard it clearly.
Then he hurried home
and I followed him.
He told the others, "You will not believe this,
but there are ONLY two moons
in the sky tonight."
He had a funny look on his face.
Then, all the others began looking into the woods.
Looking for me, no doubt!
"Only two moons, ha! Who can believe you?
We won't fall for that!" they all said to him.
They were trying to send the trick back at me!
This was clear to me!
So, I quickly wished a third moon up there
in the sky.
They looked up and saw three moons.
They had to see them!
Then one man
said out loud, "Ah, there, look up!
up there!
There is only one moon!
Well, let's go sleep on this
and in the morning
we will try and figure it out."
They all agreed, and went in their houses
to sleep.
I was left standing there
with three moons shining on me.
There were three . . . I was sure of it.

JACOB NIBEWEGENESABE
(translated from Swampy Cree by Howard A. Norman)

THE FASTEST BELT IN TOWN

Ma Bella was the fastest belt in town
Ma Bella was the fastest belt
for miles and miles around

In fact Ma Bella was the fastest belt
both in the East and in the West
nobody dared to put Ma Bella to the test

plai-plai
her belt would fly
who don't hear must cry

Milk on the floor
and Ma Bella reaching for – de belt

Slamming the door
and Ma Bella reaching for – de belt

Scribbling on the wall
and Ma Bella reaching for – de belt

Too much back-chat
and yes, Ma Bella reaching for – de belt

plai-plai
her belt would fly
who don't hear must cry

Ma Bella was the fastest belt in town
Ma Bella was the fastest belt
for miles and miles around

In fact Ma Bella was the fastest belt
both in the East and in the West
nobody dared to put Ma Bella to the test

Until one day
Ma Bella swished
missed
and lashed her own leg

That was the day Ma Bella got such a welt
That was the day Ma Bella knew exactly how it felt
That was the day Ma Bella decided to hang up her belt.

GRACE NICHOLS

SONG OF ABUSE

The one who does not love me
He will become a frog
And he will jump jump jump away.
He will become a monkey with one leg
And he will hop hop hop away.

NIGERIAN POEM

FRAGMENT

You cannot harm me,
  you cannot harm
    one who has dreamed a dream like mine

NORTH AMERICAN DAKOTA INDIAN POEM

157

THE EXECUTION

On the night of the execution
a man at the door
mistook me for the coroner.
"Press," I said.

But he didn't understand. He led me
into the wrong room
where the sheriff greeted me:
"You're late, Padre."

"You're wrong," I told him. "I'm Press."
"Yes, of course, Reverend Press."
We went down a stairway.

"Ah, Mr Ellis," said the Deputy.
"Press!" I shouted. But he shoved me
through a black curtain.
The lights were so bright
I couldn't see the faces
of the men sitting
opposite. But, thank God, I thought
they can see me!

"Look!" I cried. "Look at my face!
Doesn't anybody know me?"

Then a hood covered my head.
"Don't make it harder for us," the hangman whispered.

ALDEN NOWLAN

BREATHLESS
(Written at 21,200 feet on May 23rd)

Heart aches,
Lungs pant
The dry air
Sorry, scant.
Legs lift
And why at all?
Loose drift,
Heavy fall.
Prod the snow
Its easiest way;
A flat step
Is holiday.
Look up,
The far stone
Is many miles
Far and alone.
Grind the breath
Once more and on;
Don't look up
Till journey's done.

Must look up,
Glasses are dim.
Wrench of hand
Is breathless limb.
Pause one step,
Breath swings back;
Swallow once,
Dry throat is slack.
Then on
To the far stone;
Don't look up,
Count the steps done.
One step,
One heart-beat,
Stone no nearer
Dragging feet.
Heart aches,
Lungs pant
The dry air
Sorry, scant.

WILFRED NOYCE

CAPTAIN BUSBY

Captain Busby put his beard in his mouth and sucked it, then took it out and spat on it then put it in and sucked it then walked on down the street thinking hard.

Suddenly he put his wedding-ring in his trilby hat and put the hat on a passing kitten. Then he carefully calculated the width of the pavement with a pair of adjustable sugar-tongs. This done he knitted his brows. Then he walked on

thinking hard

PHILIP O'CONNOR

SITTING ON TREV'S BACK WALL ON THE LAST DAY OF THE HOLIDAYS TRYING TO THINK OF SOMETHING TO DO

We sit and squint on Trev's back wall
By the clothes line
Watching the shirts flap
Hearing the shirts slap
In the sunshine.
There's nothing much to do at all
But try to keep cool
And it's our last day
Of the holiday
Tomorrow we're back at school.

We keep suggesting games to play
Like Monopoly,
But you need a day
If you want to play
It properly
We played for four hours yesterday
Between rainfalls
In Trev's front room
That's like a tomb
And always smells of mothballs.

Says Trev, "Why don't we kick a ball
Over the Wasteground?"
But the weather's got
Far too hot
To run around.
John kicks his heels against the wall
Stokesy scratches his head
I head a ball
Chalk my name on the wall
While Trev pretends that he's dead.

Says John, "Let's go to the cinder track
And play speedway.
We can go by the dykes
It's not far on our bikes
I'll lead the way."
"My saddlebag's all straw at the back
Being used by blackbirds."
"And there's something unreal
About my fixed wheel
It only drives me backwards."

Trev's Granny chucks out crusts of bread
For the sparrows
While their black cat
Crouches flat
Winking in the shadows.
Trev leaps up and bangs his head
With a sudden roar.
"We could er . . .," he says.
"We could er . . .," he says.
And then sits down once more.

"Let's play Releevo on the sands,"
Says John at last.
We set out with a shout
But his mother calls out,
"It's gone half-past
Your tea's all laid, you wash your hands
They're absolutely grey."
"Oh go on Mum
Do I have to come
We were just going out to play."

Old Stokes trails home and pulls a face,
"I'll see you Trev."
"See you John."
"See you Trev."
"See you tonight the usual place."

"Yes right, all right."
"Don't forget."
"You bet."
"See you then tonight."
"See you."
"See you."
"See
You."

GARETH OWEN

MUDDY BOOTS

Trudging down the country lane,
Splodgely thlodgely plooph,
Two foot deep in slimy mud.
Fallomph Polopf Gallooph.
Hopolosplodgely go your boots,
Slopthopy gruthalamie golumph.
Then you find firm ground again,
Plonky shlonky clonky.
BUT . . . then you sink back in again,
Squelchy crathpally hodgle.

Sitting outside scraping your boots,
Sclapey gulapy criketty,
Cursing the horrible six inch slodge,
Scrapey flakey cakey.
Flakes of mud, crispling off the boots,
Crinkey splinky schlinkle.
Never again, will I venture into that
. . . Schlodgely, Flopchely, Thlodgely,
schrinkshely, slimy, grimy, squelchy, ghastly MUD!

PHILIP PADDON

163

THE OUTING

We went on an outing
to London Zoo.

We was having
a great time.

My mate Dominic
he bought a stick of rock

We went to the gorillas –
they like sweets.

My mate Dominic
he got the rock

He was messing about
with the gorillas.

My teacher said,
"NO ONE

IS ALLOWED TO MESS ABOUT WITH THE GORILLAS.
DON'T GIVE THEM SWEETS."

My friend was messing about
with the rock and the gorilla

and then the gorilla
caught the rock
and he was pulling it

and the gorilla
ate it all up –

and he wasn't allowed to.

And my teacher, Miss Grills said, to my mate,
"When you get back to school,
YOU'VE HAD IT."

NICKY PAPAPETROU

BURYING THE DOG IN THE GARDEN

When we buried
the dog in
the garden on.
the grave we put
a cross and
the tall man
next door was
cross.
"Animals have no
souls," he said.
"They must have animal
souls," we said. "No,"
he said and
shook his head.

165

"Do you need a
soul to go
to Heaven?" we
asked. He nodded
his head. "Yes,"
he said.
"That means my
hamster's not
in Heaven," said
Kevin. "Nor is
my dog," I said.
"My cat could sneak
in anywhere," said
Clare. And we thought
what a strange place Heaven
must be with
nothing to stroke
for eternity.
We were all
seven.
We decided we
did not want to
go to Heaven.
For that the
tall man next
door is to blame.

BRIAN PATTEN

STICK NO BILLS

Nevermore shall the wind's bones terrify the old clocks howling in the
    sardine-tins
Nevermore shall the feet of tables put their legs round their necks to
    imitate flies
Nevermore shall broken teeth make music
Nevermore shall loaves of bread walk about naked
Nevermore shall air-currents give orders to statues of salt
Nevermore shall the cross-bar be a railway-signal
Nevermore shall my shaved-off moustache grow again above my
    neighbour's eye
Nevermore shall the beefsteak whistle for its dog
Nevermore shall the metro ask for a drink for pity's sake
Nevermore shall cherry-stones steal latrines
because the least speck of dust the flea which looks for the ears left
    behind in taxis
the hard-boiled eggs which are so good at spying through keyholes
and all that's left of the great wall of China
are there to observe the traditions
and see that the first strawberries are respected
which look at themselves in every mirror
and would be so pleased to see a calf hanging from the butcher's stall
throw itself on to the butcher
and run away after its skin which would be so worn out
that it would see its brother through it

BENJAMIN PÉRET

MOTHS

Moths are hopeless in the air,
they are wild uncomfortable
companions to the wind,
enjoying the randomness of flight.

Moths have no face.
Smiling, I always think they
must drink light.
A cloud of them can absorb the moon.

The female moth is like the male.
When you crush it,
it doesn't bleed –
it sprinkles your hands with talcum.

WILLIAM PESKETT

MY BABY BROTHER

My baby brother is so small,
he hasn't even learned to crawl.
He's only been around a week,
and all he seems to do is bawl
and wiggle, sleep . . . and leak.

JACK PRELUTSKY

THE NEW KID ON THE BLOCK

There's a new kid on the block,
and boy, that kid is tough,
that new kid punches hard,
that new kid plays real tough,
that new kid's big and strong,
with muscles everywhere,
that new kid tweaked my arm,
that new kid pulled my hair.

That new kid likes to fight,
and picks on all the guys
that new kid scares me some,
(that new kid's twice my size),
that new kid stomped my toes,
that new kid swiped my ball,
that new kid's really bad,
I don't care for her at all.

JACK PRELUTSKY

'I CAN'T TAKE THE SUN NO MORE, MAN'

I can't take the sun no more, Man.
I buy fifty cans of cola,
I take my clothes off,
But I'm still hot.
I might as well take off my skin
It's so so so so hot, Man.
I just can't take the sun no more.
I might as well take myself apart
Before the sun melts me.
It's so so so so so so so so so
Hot, Man.
Just can't take the sun, Man.

LINVAL QUINLAND

OIL

There were **OIL**
boys and men
At sea in a boat
That wouldn't float

The boat spun round
Turned upside down
What was left then
of the **OIL**?

Turn it upside down for the answer

ENNIS REES

THE INTRUDER

Two-boots in the forest walks,
Pushing through the bracken stalks.

Vanishing like a puff of smoke,
Nimbletail flies up the oak.

Longears helter-skelter shoots
Into his house among the roots.

At work upon the highest bark,
Tapperbill knocks off to hark.

Painted-wings through sun and shade
Flounces off along the glade.

Not a creature lingers by,
When clumping Two-boots comes to pry.

JAMES REEVES

EN ROUTE

The houses sleeping their sleep of years
the sad houses
the serious houses
that like the people who inhabit them,
do not think about the trains which kiss them frenetically
in a thousand sun-sets, wishing to come in
and find relaxation for their iron-made bones
and banish from the way the inclemence* of weather   [= harshness]
which destroys everything, and the cold and
that wind that never stops.

Some of them have turned their lights on
without enthusiasm
as if they were playing at being alive
to make the trains believe that they are happy
but, like them, they're threatened by the cold
and it makes them feel uneasy when being seen by sleepy passengers
who dream about arriving, opening their doors,
turning their lights on and making the fire.

EDGARDO DURAN RESTREPO

171

CHRISTMAS STAR

I am the star
that squints in the sky

I am the sky
that squats on the cloud

I am the cloud
that squirts the earth

I am the earth
that squeezes the worm

I am the worm
that squirms under the bird

I am the bird
that squawks at the cloud

I am the cloud
that squelches in the sky

I am the sky
that squabbles with stars

I am the star
that squints in the sky

JOHN RICE

DUET

My father once had a cat named Moose,
A big TOMCAT,
And he could whistle for him
Just like you whistle for a dog.
And my father would get a chair and sit down,
And when he came in, Moose would get in his lap.
Moose would whine, and my father would say:
Moose, where have you been,
I haven't seen you all day!
And they had the conversation on the front porch,
And nobody knew what they were talking about.

FRED RICHARDSON

THE HENS

The night was coming very fast;
It reached the gate as I ran past.

The pigeons had gone to the tower of the church,
And all the hens were on their perch,

Up in the barn, and I thought I heard
A piece of a little purring word.

I stopped inside, waiting and staying,
To try to hear what the hens were saying.

They were asking something, that was plain,
Asking it over and over again.

One of them moved and turned around,
Her feathers made a ruffled sound,

A ruffled sound, like a bushful of birds,
And she said her little asking words.

She pushed her head close into her wing,
But nothing answered anything.

ELIZABETH MADOX ROBERTS

JACK BEN BENNY

Jack Ben Benny is a cat.

"How many hours shall I sit by the fire?"
Said Jack Ben Benny.
"One is too few and six is too many,"
Said Jack Ben Benny who hasn't a penny;
Said Jack Ben Benny when his eyes were grey.

"How many birds shall I eat for my breakfast?"
Said Jack Ben Benny.
"Five are a feast and one is a taste,"
Said Jack Ben Benny as he sat on a post;
Said Jack Ben Benny when his eyes were green.

"How many dogs shall I claw by the ear?"
Said Jack Ben Benny.
"One in the yard and two by the gate,"
Said Jack Ben Benny with his hair up straight;
Said Jack Ben Benny when his eyes were white.

"How many times shall I scream in the night?"
Said Jack Ben Benny.
"Once is a miaow and often is a caterwaul,"
Said Jack Ben Benny as he walked down the hall;
Said Jack Ben Benny when his eyes were red.

"And when I've done screaming where shall I purr?"
Said Jack Ben Benny.
"By Jacqueline's feet or by Jacqueline's head?"
Said Jack Ben Benny as he leaped on her bed;
Said Jack Ben Benny when his eyes were brown.

Jack Ben Benny is Jacqueline's cat.

ERIC ROLLS

MY BROTHER

my brother's on the floor roaring
my brother's on the floor roaring
why is my brother on the floor roaring?
my brother is on the floor roaring
because he's supposed to finish his beans
before he has his pudding

but he doesn't want to finish his beans
before he has his pudding

he says he wants his pudding
NOW

but they won't let him

so now my brother is on the floor roaring

they're saying
I give you one more chance to finish those beans
or you don't go to Tony's
but he's not listening
because he's on the floor roaring

he's getting told off
I'm not
I've eaten my beans
and do you know what I'm doing now?
I'm eating my pudding
and he's on the floor roaring

if he wasn't on the floor roaring
he'd see me eating my pudding
if he looked really close
he might see a little tiny smile
just at the corner of my mouth
but he's not looking.
he's on the floor roaring.

the pudding is OK
it's not wonderful
not wonderful enough
to be sitting on the floor and roaring about –
unless you're my brother

MICHAEL ROSEN

ZOO CAGE

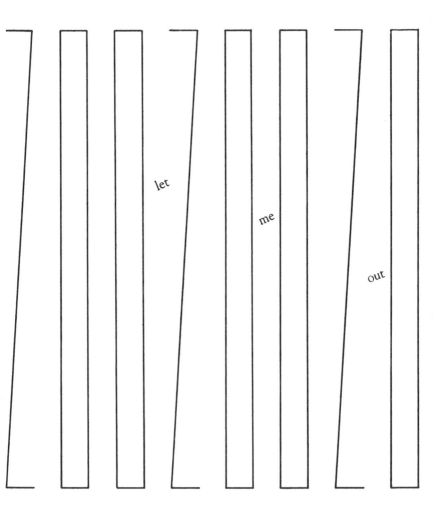

MICHAEL ROSEN

SKYSCRAPER

By day the skyscraper looms in the smoke and sun and has a soul.
Prairie and valley, streets of the city, pour people into it and they
    mingle among its twenty floors and are poured out again back to the
    streets, prairies and valleys.
It is the men and women, boys and girls so poured in and out all day that
    give the building a soul of dreams and thoughts and memories.
(Dumped in the sea or fixed in a desert, who would care for the building
    or speak its name or ask a policeman the way to it?)

Elevators slide on their cables and tubes catch letters and parcels and
    iron pipes carry gas and water in and sewage out.
Wires climb with secrets, carry light and carry words, and tell terrors
    and profits and loves – curses of men grappling plans of business and
    questions of women in plots of love.

Hour by hour the caissons reach down to the rock of the earth and hold
    the building to a turning planet.
Hour by hour the girders play as ribs and reach out and hold together
    the stone walls and floors.
Hour by hour the hand of the mason and the stuff of the mortar clinch
    the pieces and parts to the shape an architect voted.
Hour by hour the sun and the rain, the air and the rust, and the press of
    time running into centuries, play on the building inside and out and
    use it.

Men who sunk the pilings and mixed the mortar are laid in graves where
    the wind whistles a wild song without words
And so are men who strung the wires and fixed the pipes and tubes and
    those who saw it rise floor by floor.
Souls of them all are here, even the hod carrier begging at back doors
    hundreds of miles away and the bricklayer who went to state's prison
    for shooting another man while drunk.
(One man fell from a girder and broke his neck at the end of a straight
    plunge – he is here – his soul has gone into the stones of the
    building.)

On the office doors from tier to tier – hundreds of names and each name standing for a face written across with a dead child, a passionate lover, a driving ambition for a million dollar business or a lobster's ease of life.

Behind the signs on the doors they work and the walls tell nothing from room to room.

Ten-dollar-a-week stenographers take letters from corporation officers, lawyers, efficiency engineers, and tons of letters go bundled from the building to all ends of the earth.

Smiles and tears of each office girl go into the soul of the building just the same as the master-men who rule the building.

Hands of clocks turn to noon hours and each floor empties its men and women who go away and eat and come back to work.

Toward the end of the afternoon all work slackens and all jobs go slower as the people feel day closing on them.

One by one the floors are emptied. . . The uniformed elevator men are gone. Pails clang. . . Scrubbers work, talking in foreign tongues. Broom and water and mop clean from the floors human dust and spit, and machine grime of the day.

Spelled in electric fire on the roof are words telling miles of houses and people where to buy a thing for money. The sign speaks till midnight.

Darkness on the hallways. Voices echo. Silence holds. . . Watchmen walk slow from floor to floor and try the doors. Revolvers bulge from their hip pockets. . . Steel safes stand in corners. Money is stacked in them.

A young watchman leans at a window and sees the lights of barges butting their way across a harbour, nets of red and white lanterns in a railroad yard, and a span of glooms splashed with lines of white and blurs of crosses and clusters over the sleeping city.

By night the skyscraper looms in the smoke and the stars and has a soul.

CARL SANDBURG

HARD CHEESE

The grown-ups are all safe,
Tucked up inside,
Where they belong.

They doze into the telly,
Bustle through the washing-up,
Snore into the fire,
Rustle through the paper.

They're all there,
Out of harm's way.

Now it's *our* street:
All the back-yards,
All the gardens,
All the shadows,
All the dark corners,
All the privet-hedges,
All the lamp-posts,
All the door-ways.

Here is an important announcement:
The army of occupation
Is confined to barracks.
Hooray.

We're the natives.
We creep out at night,
Play everywhere,
Swing on *all* the lamp-posts,
Slit your gizzard?

Then, about nine o'clock,
They send out search-parties.

We can hear them coming.
And we crouch
In the garden-sheds,
Behind the dust-bins,
Up the alley-ways,
Inside the dust-bins,
Or stand stock-still,
And pull ourselves in,
As thin as a pin,
Behind the lamp-posts.

And they stand still,
And peer into the dark.
They take a deep breath –
You can hear it for miles –

And, then, they bawl,
They shout, they caterwaul:
"J-i-i-i-i-mmeeee!"
"Timeforbed. D'youhearme?"
"M-a-a-a-a-reeee!"

"J-o-o-o-o-o-hnneeee!"
"S-a-a-a-a-a-mmeeee!"
"Mary!" "Jimmy!"
"Johnny!" "Sammy!"
Like cats. With very big mouths.
Then we give ourselves up,
Prisoners-of-war.
Till tomorrow night.

But just you wait.
One of these nights
We'll hold out,
We'll lie doggo,
And wait, and wait,
Till they just give up
And mumble
And go to bed.
You just wait.
They'll see!

JUSTIN ST JOHN

IN THE PINK

So Davies wrote: "This leaves me in the pink."
Then scrawled his name: "Your loving sweetheart, Willie."
With crosses for a hug. He'd had a drink
Of rum and tea; and, though the barn was chilly,
For once his blood ran warm; he had pay to spend.
Winter was passing; soon the year would mend.

But he couldn't sleep that night; stiff in the dark
He groaned and thought of Sundays at the farm,
And how he'd go as cheerful as a lark
In his best suit, to wander arm in arm
With brown-eyed Gwen, and whisper in her ear
The simple, silly things she liked to hear.

And then he thought: tomorrow night we trudge
Up to the trenches, and my boots are rotten.
Five miles of stodgy clay and freezing sludge,
And everything but wretchedness forgotten.
To-night he's in the pink; but soon he'll die.
And still the war goes on – *he* don't know why.

SIEGFRIED SASSOON

HIDE AND SEEK

Call out. Call loud: "I'm ready! Come and find me!"
The sacks in the toolshed smell like the seaside.
They'll never find you in this salty dark,
But be careful that your feet aren't sticking out.
Wiser not to risk another shout.
The floor is cold. They'll probably be searching
The bushes near the swing. Whatever happens
You mustn't sneeze when they come prowling in.
And here they are, whispering at the door;
You've never heard them sound so hushed before.

Don't breathe. Don't move. Stay dumb. Hide in your blindness.
They're moving closer, someone stumbles, mutters;
Their words and laughter scuffle, and they're gone.
But don't come out just yet; they'll try the lane
And then the greenhouse and back here again.
They must be thinking that you're very clever,
Getting more puzzled as they search all over.
It seems a long time since they went away.
Your legs are stiff, the cold bites through your coat;
The dark damp smell of sand moves in your throat.
It's time to let them know that you're the winner.
Push off the sacks. Uncurl and stretch. That's better!
Out of the shed and call to them: "I've won!
Here I am! Come and own up I've caught you!"
The darkening garden watches. Nothing stirs.
The bushes hold their breath; the sun is gone.
Yes, here you are. But where are they who sought you?

VERNON SCANNELL

185

PRISONER AND JUDGE

1   The prisoner was walking round and round the prison yard.
He had a low forehead and cruel eyes;
You couldn't trust him anywhere.

He dressed up as a judge; he put on a wig and robes
And sat in court in the judge's place.
And everyone said:
   "What a deep forehead he has, what learned eyes!
   How wise he looks!
   You could trust him anywhere."

2   The judge was sitting in court in the judge's place.
He had a deep forehead and learned eyes;
You could trust him anywhere.

He dressed up as a prisoner; he put on prisoner's clothes
And walked round and round the prison yard.
And everyone said:
   "What a low forehead he has, what cruel eyes!
   How stupid he looks!
   You couldn't trust him anywhere."

IAN SERRAILLIER

SHYLOCK'S LAMENT
(from *The Merchant of Venice*)

I am a Jew. Hath not a Jew eyes? hath not a Jew hands, organs, dimensions, senses, affections, passions? fed with the same food, hurt with the same weapons, subject to the same diseases, healed by the same means, warmed and cooled by the same winter and summer as a Christian is? – if you prick us do we not bleed? if you tickle us do we not laugh? if you poison us do we not die?

WILLIAM SHAKESPEARE

CALIBAN'S CURSE
(from *The Tempest*)

This island's mine, by Sycorax my mother,
Which thou tak'st from me. When thou cam'st first,
Thou strok'st me, and made much of me; wouldst give me
Water with berries in't; and teach me how
To name the bigger light, and how the less,
That burn by day and night: and then I lov'd thee,
And show'd thee all the qualities o' th' isle,
The fresh springs, brine-pits, barren place and fertile:
Curs'd be I that did so! All the charms
Of Sycorax, toads, beetles, bats, light on you!
For I am all the subjects that you have,
Which first was mine own King: and here you sty me
In this hard rock, whiles you do keep from me
The rest o' th' island.

WILLIAM SHAKESPEARE

A SONG

A widow bird sate mourning for her love
   Upon a wintry bough;
The frozen wind crept on above,
   The freezing stream below.

There was no leaf upon the forest bare,
   No flower upon the ground,
And little motion in the air
   Except the mill-wheel's sound.

PERCY BYSSHE SHELLEY

'ON NIGHTS WHEN HAIL'

On nights when hail
falls noisily
on bamboo leaves,
I completely hate
to sleep alone.

IZUMI SHIKIBU
(translated by Willis Barnstone)

9 YEARS OLD

Rachel make your bed up
Rachel brush your teeth
Rachel you'll get fat
If you eat too many sweets

Rachel put your glasses on
Rachel move your clothes
Rachel you still go around
As if you're 3 years old

What's that towel doing on the floor
Rachel pick it up
What's that underneath your bed, Rachel?
A saucer and a cup

Biscuit crumbs, sweetie papers
Books of every kind
If I look under the blankets
Heaven knows what I will find

Rachel it is way past nine
Rachel go to bed
Rachel have you listened
To anything I've said

I say the same things every day
But Rachel, do you hear?
Rachel do you understand?
Rachel do you care?

LORRAINE SIMEON

OBSTACLES

I can't take no more, I can't stand it
I tell you, I've really had enough
How many times has this been said
When the going begins to get tough

So you turn your back on that problem
And for a while you're feeling strong
But you are right back where you started
When the next one comes along

LORRAINE SIMEON

THE RIVER GOD

I may be smelly and I may be old,
Rough in my pebbles, reedy in my pools,
But where my fish float by I bless their swimming
And I like the people to bathe in me, especially women.
But I can drown the fools
Who bathe too close to the weir, contrary to rules.
And they take a long time drowning
As I throw them up now and then in a spirit of clowning.
Hi yih, yippity-yap, merrily I flow,
O I may be an old foul river but I have plenty of go.
Once there was a lady who was too bold
She bathed in me by the tall black cliff where the water runs cold,
So I brought her down here
To be my beautiful dear.
Oh will she stay with me will she stay
This beautiful lady, or will she go away?
She lies in my beautiful deep river bed with many a weed
To hold her, and many a waving reed.
Oh who would guess what a beautiful white face lies there

190

Waiting for me to smooth and wash away the fear
She looks at me with. Hi yih, do not let her
Go. There is no one on earth who does not forget her
Now. They say I am a foolish old smelly river
But they do not know of my wide original bed
Where the lady waits, with her golden sleepy head.
If she wishes to go I will not forgive her.

STEVIE SMITH

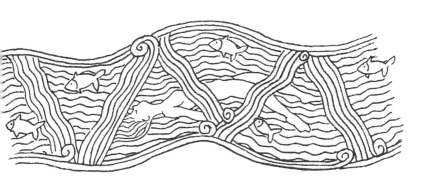

THE STARS

When night comes
I stand on the stairway and listen,
the stars are swarming in the garden
and I am standing in the dark.
Listen, a star fell with a tinkle!
Do not go out on the grass with bare feet;
my garden is full of splinters.

EDITH SÖDERGRAN
(translated by David McDuff)

THE WILLOW

Of all the trees in our village,
The willow
Beyond the potato field
Had no luck –
They made a rubbish dump there.

Well, in the first place, it's not known whose she was,
Or who planted her there, and why –
We don't know.
If around other
Quite domestic and quite seemly willows,
It is quite well swept and clean, as in a hut –
By that ill-conceived one
There's a pile of god-knows-what.
People bring scrap iron,
Galoshes, boots.
Quite useless now, of course,
(If they were good for anything at all they wouldn't bring them)
And when the cat dies, they dump it by the tree.
So encircled is the poor willow
With torn rags and rotting cats
That it is better now to give her a wide berth.

But still, when May comes,
Up to her knees in muck
She suddenly begins to gild herself peacefully.
She doesn't care a rap about the ripped galoshes,
The jars and tins and rags of clothes.
She flowers, as all her earthly sisters
Flower –
With a modest flowering,
With the purest, most innocent of flowers
Opening primordially to the sun.

And it shines. And everything smells of honey.
It happens that bees fly to her
In spite of the refuse at her base,
Bear away the flowers' translucent honey
To people who abuse trees.

VLADIMIR SOLOUKHIN
(translated by Daniel Weissbort)

SUMMER SHOWER

Hunched together at the bus-stop
north of Serpent River,

three Indian girls,
being soaked to the skin
from the downpour, stare hard

as our cars flash by,
not with envy
or with anger, certainly,

but more resignation
that in this world
every time it rains
some people will come out
wet and some dry

with no-one in between.

RAYMOND SOUSTER

BISHOP HATTO

The summer and autumn had been so wet,
That in winter the corn was growing yet,
'Twas a piteous sight to see all around
The grain lie rotting on the ground.

Every day the starving poor
Crowded around Bishop Hatto's door,
For he had a plentiful last-year's store,
And all the neighbourhood could tell
His granaries were furnished well.

At last Bishop Hatto appointed a day
To quiet the poor without delay;
He bade them to his great barn repair,
And they should have food for the winter there.

Rejoiced such tidings good to hear,
The poor folk flocked from far and near;
The great barn was full as it could hold
Of women and children, and young and old.

Then when he saw it could hold no more,
Bishop Hatto he made fast the door;
And while for mercy on Christ they call,
He set fire to the barn and burnt them all.

"I' faith, 'tis an excellent bonfire!" quoth he,
"And the country is greatly obliged to me,
For ridding it in these times forlorn
Of rats that only consume the corn."

So then to his palace returned he,
And he sat down to supper merrily,
And he slept that night like an innocent man;
But Bishop Hatto never slept again.

In the morning as he entered the hall
Where his picture hung against the wall,
A sweat like death all over him came,
For the rats had eaten it out of the frame.

As he looked there came a man from his farm,
He had a countenance white with alarm;
"My Lord, I opened your granaries this morn,
And the rats had eaten all your corn."

Another came running presently,
And he was pale as pale could be,
"Fly! my Lord Bishop, fly!" quoth he,
"Ten thousand rats are coming this way –
The Lord forgive you for yesterday!"

"I'll go to my tower on the Rhine," replied he,
"'Tis the safest place in Germany;
The walls are high and the shores are steep,
And the stream is strong and the water deep."

Bishop Hatto fearfully hastened away,
And he crossed the Rhine without delay,
And reached his tower, and barred with care
All windows, doors, and loop-holes there.

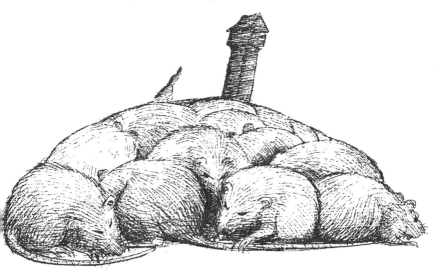

He laid him down and closed his eyes; –
But soon a scream made him arise,
He stared and saw two eyes of flame
On his pillow from whence the screaming came.

He listened and looked – it was only the cat;
But the Bishop he grew more fearful for that,
For she sat screaming, mad with fear
At the army of rats that were drawing near.

For they have swum over the river so deep,
And they have climbed the shores so steep,
And up the tower their way is bent,
To do the work for which they were sent.

They are not to be told by the dozen or score,
By thousands they come, and by myriads and more,
Such numbers had never been heard of before,
Such a judgment had never been witnessed of yore.

Down on his knees the Bishop fell
And faster and faster his beads did he tell,
As louder and louder drawing near
The gnawing of their teeth he could hear.

And in at the window and in at the door,
And through the walls helter-skelter they pour,
And down from the ceiling, and up through the floor,
From the right and the left, from behind and before,
From within and without, from above and below,
And all at once to the Bishop they go.

They have whetted their teeth against the stones,
And now they pick the Bishop's bones;
They gnawed the flesh from every limb,
For they were sent to do judgment on him!

ROBERT SOUTHEY

THE POET'S BOYHOOD

Whilome in youth, when flowered my joyful spring,
Like swallow swift I wand'red here and there;
For heat of heedless lust me so did sting,
That I of doubted danger had no fear:
    I went the wastefull woods and forest wide,
    Withouten dread of wolves to been espied.

I wont to range amid the mazy thicket,
And gather nuts to make me Christmas game,
And joyèd oft to chase the trembling pricket*,   [= male fallow deer]
Or hunt the heartless hare till she were tame.
    What wreakèd I of winter ages waste? –
    Tho' deemèd I my spring would ever last.

How often have I scaled the craggy oak,
All to dislodge the raven of her nest?
How have I wearièd with many a stroke
The stately walnut-tree, the while the rest
    Under the tree fell all for nuts at strife?
    For ylike to me was liberty and life.

EDMUND SPENSER

JESSEL'S SONG

I like mas *   [= carnival]
I like playing
with my class
jumping up and down
the street
look I feeling so sweet

I like mas
I like the steel
and the brass
jumping up and down
look I feeling so sweet

And if you see me
how I looking sharp
with meh costume
up to mark
playing mas in the city
oh how happy I will be

I like mas
I like playing
with my class
jumping up and down
the street

look I feeling so sweet.

EINTOU PEARL SPRINGER

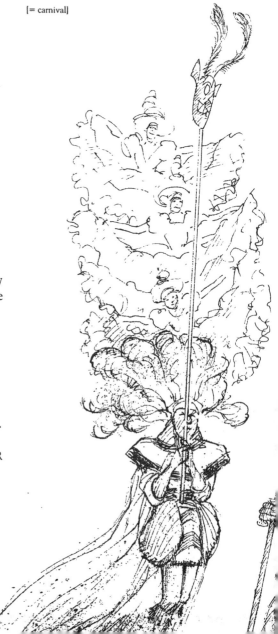

THE MAIN-DEEP

The long, rolling,
Steady-pouring,
Deep-trenchèd
Green billow:

The wide-topped,
Unbroken,
Green-glacid,
Slow-sliding,

Cold-flushing,
On – on – on –
Chill-rushing,
Hush-hushing,

Hush – hushing . . .

JAMES STEPHENS

ESCAPE AT BEDTIME

The lights from the parlour and kitchen shone out
   Through the blinds and the windows and bars;
And high overhead and all moving about,
   There were thousands of millions of stars.
There ne'er were such thousands of leaves on a tree,
   Nor of people in church or the Park,
As the crowds of the stars that looked down upon me,
   And that glittered and winked in the dark.

The Dog, and the Plough, and the Hunter, and all,
   And the star of the sailor, and Mars,
These shone in the sky, and the pail by the wall
   Would be half full of water and stars.
They saw me at last, and they chased me with cries,
   And they soon had me packed into bed;
But the glory kept shining and bright in my eyes,
   And the stars going round in my head.

ROBERT LOUIS STEVENSON

OLD DAN'L

Out of his cottage to the sun
Bent double comes old Dan'l,
His chest all over cotton wool,
His back all over flannel.

"Winter will finish him," they've said
Each winter now for ten:
But come the first warm day of Spring
Old Dan'l's out again.

L. A. G. STRONG

SLIPS

I was sitting watching the tele,
I was interested in the film –
It was the Magnificent Five –
When my Mum said:
"Switch the door off and shut the light."

My brother Simon has a bullet
Which he wears on a thong around his neck.
He started wearing this at night, in bed,
As well as during the day time.
Mum and Dad were both worried about this.
Mum was going on and on about it and she said:
"If you wake up dead in the morning . . .!"

When my brother was six,
He'd been watching an operation on TV
About a lady who was having her kidneys removed.

201

Later he was trying to tell me about it and said:
"Jamie, you know that lady who
Had her mushrooms removed . . ."

One day our mam was in a rush
To make the beds, make the dinner
And get out.
She said:
"Go upstairs
And wash the door
And shut your face."

Matthew Drury said,
After it had been snowing,
"I've just been snowing throwballs."

My teacher said:
"Get the board and
Put the date on the chalk."

from the SUNDAY TIMES MAGAZINE
(collated by Michael Rosen)

A DESCRIPTION OF THE MORNING

Now hardly here and there an hackney-coach
Appearing, showed the ruddy morn's approach.
Now Betty from her Master's bed had flown,
And softly stole to discompose her own.
The slipshod 'Prentice from his Master's door,
Had pared the street, and sprinkled round the floor.
Now Moll had whirled her mop with dextrous* airs,   [= skilful]
Prepared to scrub the entry and the stairs.
The Youth with broomy stumps began to trace
The kennel edge, where wheels had worn the place.
The Smallcoal-man was heard with cadence deep,
Till drowned in shriller notes of Chimney-sweep.
Duns* at his Lordship's gate began to meet;   [= those owed money]
And Brickdust Moll had screamed through half a street.
The Turnkey* now his flock returning sees,   [= jailor]
Duly let out a-nights to steal for fees.
The watchful Bailiffs take their silent stands;
And Schoolboys lag with satchels in their hands.

JONATHAN SWIFT

HE DID NOT JUMP DOWN FROM THE THIRD FLOOR

The Second World War.
Warsaw.
Last night they dropped bombs
on Theatre Square.

My father's workshop
is in Theatre Square.
All his paintings, work
of forty years.

203

This morning he went
to Theatre Square.
He realized.

His workshop had
no roof
no walls
no floor.

My father did not jump down
from the third floor.
My father just began all over again.

ANNA ŚWIRSZCZYŃSKA
(translated by Susan Bassnett and Piotr Kuhiwczak)

I WONDER IF SHE KNOWS

There was a purebred siamese cat
drinking from a dirty puddle
on the street
I think it lives
in that house with the well kept lawn
The girl that feeds her purina dainties
and goat's milk
is probably fixing her velvet pillow
for her sleep
and I wonder if she knows
her cat is drinking ordinary rain water
off the street.

SALI TAGLIAMONTE

from STRAY BIRDS

The bird wishes it were a cloud;
The cloud wishes it were a bird.

The woodcutter's axe begged for its handle from the tree;
The tree gave it.

The stars are not afraid to appear like fireflies.

The cobweb pretends to catch dewdrops and catches flies.

The canal loves to think that rivers exist
solely to supply it with water.

RABINDRANATH TAGORE

VOCATION

When the gong sounds ten in the morning and I walk to school by
our lane,
  Every day I meet the hawker crying, "Bangles, crystal bangles!"
  There is nothing to hurry him on, there is no road he must take,
no place he must go to, no time when he must come home.
  I wish I were a hawker, spending my day in the road,
crying, "Bangles, crystal bangles!"

When at four in the afternoon I come back from the school,
  I can see through the gate of that house the gardener digging
the ground.
  He does what he likes with his spade, he soils his clothes with dust,
nobody takes him to task if he gets baked in the sun or gets wet.
  I wish I were a gardener digging away at the garden with nobody
to stop me from digging.

Just as it gets dark in the evening and my mother sends me to bed,
  I can see through my open window the watchman walking up
and down.
  The lane is dark and lonely, and the street-lamp stands like a
giant with one red eye in its head.
  The watchman swings his lantern and walks with his shadow
at his side, and never once goes to bed in his life.
  I wish I were a watchman walking the streets all night, chasing
the shadows with my lantern.

RABINDRANATH TAGORE

HILL ROLLING

I kind of exploded inside,
and joy shot out of me.
I began my roll down the grassy hill.
I bent my knees up small, took a deep breath
and I was off.

My arms shot out sideways.
I gathered speed.
My eyes squinted.
Sky and grass, dazzle and dark.

I went on forever,
My arms were covered with dents,
holes, squashed grass.
Before I knew it I was at the bottom.
The game was over.
The door of the classroom closed behind me.
I can smell chalk dust, and hear the voice of teacher,
to make me forget my hill.

ANDREW TAYLOR

A LAMB

Yes, I saw a lamb where they've built a new housing estate, where cars are parked in garages, where streets have names like Fern Hill Crescent

I saw a lamb where television aerials sprout from chimneypots, where young men gun their motorbikes, where mothers watch from windows between lace curtains

I saw a lamb, I tell you, where lawns in front are neatly clipped, where cabbages and cauliflowers grow in back gardens, where doors and gates are newly painted

I saw a lamb, there in the dusk, the evening fires just lit, a scent of coal-smoke on the air, the sky faintly bruised by the sunset

yes, I saw it, I was troubled. I wanted to ask someone, anyone, something, anything . . .

a man in a raincoat coming home from work but he was in a hurry. I went in at the next gate and rang the doorbell, and rang, but no one answered.

I noticed that the lights in the house were out. Someone shouted at me from an upstairs window next door, "They're on holiday. What do you want?" And I turned away because I wanted nothing

but a lamb in a green field.

GAEL TURNBULL

PROCESS

What was I doing
When
Everyone was saying "Hail"?
I was also saying "Hail,"
And was afraid,
     as everyone was.

What was I doing
When
Everyone was saying,
"Aziz is my enemy"?
I too said,
"Aziz is my enemy."

What was I doing
When everybody was saying,
"Don't open your mouth"?
I also said,
"Don't open your mouth,
Say
What everyone says."

The shouts of "Hail" have ceased.
Aziz has been killed;
Mouths have been silenced.

Bewildered, everyone asks
"How did it happen?"
As others ask
So I ask,
"How did it happen?"

SHRIKANT VERMA
(translated by Vishnu Khare)

NIGHT FUN

I hear eating.
I hear drinking.
I hear music.
I hear laughter.
Fun is something
Grownups never have
Before my bedtime.
Only after.

JUDITH VIORST

SECRETS

Anne told Beth.
And Beth told me.
And I am telling you.
But don't tell Sue –
You know she can't
Keep secrets.

JUDITH VIORST

REMEMBER ME?

What will they say
When I've gone away:
He was handsome? He was fun?
He shared his gum? He wasn't
Too dumb or too smart? He
Played a good game of volley ball?
Or will they only say
He stepped in the dog doo
At Jimmy Altman's party?

JUDITH VIORST

AN OMEN
(from *The Aeneid*)

A Golden Eagle, Jupiter's bird, high up in the red sky
was chasing a flock of water-birds.
They screeched and screamed out loud
as they flew ahead of it. Suddenly it swooped down to the water
and greedily seized a magnificent swan in its hook-like claws.
The Italians grew tense as they watched.
Now the whole flock of water-birds
wheeled and turned, still screaming – an amazing sight to see –
and darkening the sky with their wings,
closed up into a cloud and mobbed
the eagle driving it ahead of them, until overwhelmed by their fury
and the sheer weight of its load, it weakened, dropping the swan
into the river below and fled to the cover of a cloud.

VIRGIL
(translated by C. Day Lewis)

SNAKE
(from *The Aeneid*)

When a snake has been caught on the hump of a high road
a bronze wheel running across it, or a traveller smashing it hard with
a stone and leaving it there, crushed and half dead, the serpent
makes hopeless attempts to escape, wriggling its long body –
part of it still defiant, eyes blazing, the neck reared upright
and hissing; while part of it, crippled by injury drags,
lashing itself into knots and writhing back on its own coils.

VIRGIL
(translated by C. Day Lewis)

THE FEET

At night, the feet become lonely.

All day they have considerable importance:
are carefully dressed in shoes
and ready at any moment to stand,
move around, take the weight of the body.
Even when the body is sitting, sometimes
the feet depress certain pedals
to control an automobile travelling at tremendous speeds
for hundreds of miles.

But at night
even their socks are taken away.
The feet are made to lie down naked
in a part of the bed no one visits.
All night they lie there, with nothing to do.

Hidden away in the darkness
under sheets and blankets
no wonder the two abandoned feet
begin a clumsy relationship.

212

One foot
suddenly crosses the ankle of the other
like a blind horse putting his head over the neck of another blind horse.
The feet lie like this, touching all night
– stiff, self-conscious, not saying a word.

TOM WAYMAN

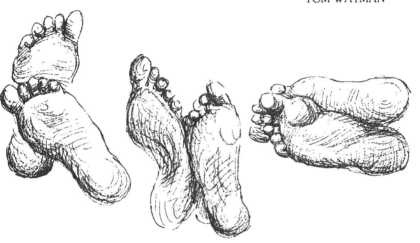

WHEN I HEARD THE LEARN'D ASTRONOMER

When I heard the learn'd astronomer,
When the proofs, the figures, were ranged in columns before me,
When I was shown the charts and diagrams, to add, divide, and
    measure them,
When I sitting heard the astronomer where he lectured with much
    applause in the lecture-room,
How soon unaccountable I became tired and sick,
Till rising and gliding out I wander'd off by myself,
In the mystical moist night-air, and from time to time,
Look'd up in perfect silence at the stars.

WALT WHITMAN

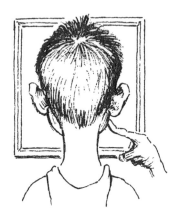

WHISKERS

Dad! When will I be able to shave?
When will I have whiskers like you?
DAD!!
When will I be ready to shave?
Really!
Fifteen!
Is that true?
Dad!
Will you help me when I have to start?
How far do you go down your neck?
Dad!
What's that red stuff, there on your throat?
Dad!
Don't shout!

OH! HECK!!! . . .

BARRIE WHITTLE

NOT BEING ABLE TO SLEEP

The worst thing about
not being able to sleep
I think
is
when suddenly you realize
that you're not going to be able
to sleep.

SIV WIDERBERG

PROLETARIAN PORTRAIT

A big young bareheaded woman
in an apron

Her hair slicked back standing
on the street

One stockinged foot toeing
the sidewalk

Her shoe in her hand. Looking
intently into it

She pulls out the paper insole
to find the nail

That has been hurting her

WILLIAM CARLOS WILLIAMS

215

YOU AND I SHALL GO

It is above that you and I shall go;
Along the Milky Way you and I shall go;
Along the flower trail you and I shall go;
Picking flowers on our way you and I shall go.

WINTU

ICE

was the first time
anyone remembers it happening

the fields froze
in our village
in south china

we broke some
not knowing what it was
and took it to the junk peddler

he thought it was glass
and traded us a penny
for it

he wrapped it up
in old cloth and placed it
on top of his basket

of course
the noon day sun melted it

by the time
we came back with more
he had gotten wise

JIM WONG-CHU

from THE PRELUDE, BOOK 1

And in the frosty season, when the sun
Was set, and visible for many a mile
The cottage windows through the twilight blaz'd,
I heeded not the summons: – happy time
It was, indeed, for all of us; to me
It was a time of rapture: clear and loud
The village clock tolled six; I wheeled about,
Proud and exulting, like an untired horse,
That cares not for his home. All shod with steel,
We hissed along the polished ice in games
Confederate, imitative of the chase
And woodland pleasures, the resounding horn,
The pack loud bellowing, and the hunted hare.
So through the darkness and the cold we flew,
And not a voice was idle; with the din,
Meanwhile the precipices rang aloud,
The leafless trees, and every icy crag
Tinkled like iron, while the distant hills
Into the tumult sent an alien sound
Of melancholy, not unnoticed, while the stars,
Eastward, were sparkling clear, and in the west
The orange sky of evening died away.

WILLIAM WORDSWORTH

DAVE DIRT WAS ON THE 259

Dave Dirt was on the 259
(Down Seven Sisters Road it goes),
And since he'd nothing else to do
He stuck his ticket up his nose,

He shoved his pen-top in his ear,
He pulled three hairs out of his head,
He ate a page out of his book,
He held his breath till he went red,

He stuck his tongue out at the queue,
He found a nasty scab to pick,
He burped and blew a raspberry,
He imitated being sick,

He stuck a piece of bubblegum
Inside a dear old lady's bonnet.
If you should catch the 259
Make sure that Dave Dirt isn't on it!

KIT WRIGHT

THE SONG OF WANDERING AENGUS

I went out to the hazel wood,
Because a fire was in my head,
And cut and peeled a hazel wand,
And hooked a berry to a thread,
And when white moths were on the wing,
And moth-like stars were flickering out,
I dropped the berry in a stream
And caught a little silver trout.

218

When I had laid it on the floor
I went to blow the fire a-flame,
But something rustled on the floor,
And someone called me by my name:
It had become a glimmering girl
With apple blossoms in her hair
Who called me by my name and ran
And faded through the brightening air.

Though I am old with wandering
Through hollow lands and hilly lands,
I will find out where she has gone,
And kiss her lips and take her hands;
And walk among long dappled grass,
And pluck till time and times are done,
The silver apples of the moon,
The golden apples of the sun.

WILLIAM BUTLER YEATS

PYTHON

Swaggering prince
Giant among snakes.
They say python has no house.
I heard it a long time ago
And I laughed and laughed and laughed.
For who owns the ground under the lemon grass?
Who owns the ground under the elephant grass?
Who owns the swamp – father of rivers?
Who owns the stagnant pool – father of waters?

Because they never walk hand in hand
People say that snakes only walk singly.
But just imagine
Suppose the viper walks in front
The green mamba follows
And the python creeps rumbling behind –
Who will be brave enough
To wait for them?

YORUBA POEM

A DOG

I am alone.
Someone is raking leaves
outside
and there is one yellow leaf
on the black branch
brushing the window.
Suddenly a cold wet nose
nuzzles
my empty hand.

CHARLOTTE ZOLOTOW

BALLADS

THE BALLAD OF HOLLIS BROWN

Hollis Brown
He lived on the outside of town
Hollis Brown
He lived on the outside of town
With his wife and five children
And his cabin fallin' down

You looked for work and money
And you walked a rugged mile
You looked for work and money
And you walked a rugged mile
Your children are so hungry
That they don't know how to smile

Your baby's eyes look crazy
They're a-tuggin' at your sleeve
Your baby's eyes look crazy
They're a-tuggin' at your sleeve
You walk the floor and wonder why
With every breath you breathe

The rats have got your flour
Bad blood it got your mare
The rats have got your flour
Bad blood it got your mare
If there's anyone that knows
Is there anyone that cares?

You prayed to the Lord above
Oh please send you a friend

You prayed to the Lord above
Oh please send you a friend
Your empty pockets tell yuh
That you ain't a-got no friend

Your babies are crying louder
It's pounding on your brain
Your babies are crying louder now
It's pounding on your brain
Your wife's screams are stabbin' you
Like the dirty drivin' rain

Your grass it is turning black
There's no water in your well
Your grass it is turning black
There's no water in your well
You spent your last lone dollar
On seven shotgun shells

Way out in the wilderness
A cold coyote calls
Way out in the wilderness
A cold coyote calls
Your eyes fix on the shotgun
That's hangin' on the wall

Your brain is a-bleedin'
And your legs can't seem to stand
Your brain is a-bleedin'
And your legs can't seem to stand
Your eyes fix on the shotgun
That you're holdin' in your hand

There's seven breezes a-blowin'
All around the cabin door
There's seven breezes a-blowin'
All around the cabin door
Seven shots ring out
Like the ocean's pounding roar

There's seven people dead
On a South Dakota farm
There's seven people dead
On a South Dakota farm
Somewhere in the distance
There's seven new people born

BOB DYLAN

CASEY JONES

Come all you rounders, I want you to hear
The story of a brave engineer*;   [= train driver]
Casey Jones was the rounder's name,
On a big eight-wheeler of a mighty fame.

Chorus:
Casey Jones, he pushed on the throttler,
Casey Jones was a brave engineer,
Come on, Casey, and blow the whistler,
Blow the whistle so they all can hear.

Now Casey said, "Before I die
There's one more train that I want to try,
And I will try ere many a day
The Union Pacific and the Santa Fé."

223

Caller called Casey about half past four,
He kissed his wife at the station door,
Climbed in his cab and was on his way,
"I've got my chance on the Santa Fe."

Down the slope he went on the fly,
Heard the fireman say, "You've got a white eye."
Well, the switchman knew by the engine's moan
That the man at the throttle was Casey Jones.

The rain was a-pounding down like lead,
The railroad track was a river bed,
They slowed her down to a thirty-mile gait,
And the south-bound mail was eight hours late.

Fireman says, "Casey, you're running too fast,
You run the black board the last station you passed."
Casey says, "I believe we'll make it through,
For the steam's much better than I ever knew."

Around the curve comes a passenger train,
Her headlight was shining in his eyes through the rain,
Casey blew the whistle a mighty blast
But the locomotive was a-comin' fast.

The locomotives met in the middle of the hill,
In a head-on tangle that's bound to kill,
He tried to do his duty, the yard men said,
But Casey Jones was scalded dead.

Headaches and heartaches and all kinds of pain
They all ride along with the railroad train,
Stories of brave men, noble and grand,
Belong to the life of the railroad man.

ANON.

DICK TURPIN AND THE LAWYER

As Turpin was riding across the moor
There he saw a lawyer riding on before.
Turpin, riding up to him, said, "Are you not afraid
To meet Dick Turpin, that mischievous blade?"
   Singing Eh ro, Turpin I ro.

Says Turpin to the lawyer for to be cute,
"I hid my money into my boot."
Says the lawyer to Turpin, "He can't find mine,
For I hid it in the cape of my coat behind."
   Singing Eh ro, Turpin I ro.

They rode along together to the foot of the hill,
When Turpin bid the lawyer to stand still,
Saying, "The cape of your coat it must come off,
For my horse is in want of a new saddle-cloth."
   Singing Eh ro, Turpin I ro.

Turpin robbed the lawyer of all his store;
He told him to go home and he would get more;
"And the very first town you do come in
You can tell them you was robbed by Dick Turpin."
   Singing Eh ro, Turpin I ro.

ANON.

POLLY VAUGHAN

Come all you young fellows that handle a gun,
Beware how you shoot when the night is coming on,
For young Jimmy met his true love, and took her for a swan,
And he shot her and he killed her by the setting of the sun.

Then home ran young Jimmy with his dog and his gun,
Crying: "Uncle, dear uncle, have you heard what I've done?
I've shot my own true love instead of a swan
As she sat in her white apron at the setting of the sun."

Now the girls of this country they will be very glad
To hear the sad news that young Polly is dead.
You may take all those cruel girls and set them in a row,
And her beauty would shine among them like a fountain of snow.

Well, the trial came on and Polly's ghost did appear,
Crying: "Uncle, dear uncle, let Jimmy go clear,
For my apron was thrown round me and he took me for a swan,
Or he never would have shot at his own Polly Vaughan."

ANON.

226

LIMERICKS

There was a young man of Devizes,
Whose ears were of different sizes.
  One was so small
  It was no use at all,
But the other was huge and won prizes.

There once was a plesiosaurus,
Who lived when the world was all porous;
  But it fainted with shame,
  When it first heard its name,
And departed long ages before us.

A sensitive girl called O'Neill
Went on the fairground Big Wheel;
  When half-way around,
  She looked down at the ground,
And it cost her a two-dollar meal.

There was an old Justice named Percival,
Who said, "I suppose you'll get worse if I'll
  Send you to jail,
  So I'll put you on bail."
Now wasn't Judge Percival merciful?

I'd rather have fingers than toes;
I'd rather have ears than a nose;
   And as for my hair,
   I'm glad that it's there.
I'll be awfully sad when it goes.

GELETT BURGESS

There was an old poacher called Bruce
Whose belt was always too loose.
One day in the town
His trousers fell down,
And out came three cats and a goose.

MICHAEL PALIN

RIDDLES IN RHYME

(All Anon. unless author given)

Legs I have got, yet seldom do I walk;
I backbite many, yet I never talk;
In secret places most I seek to hide me,
For he who feeds me never can abide me.

'Tis true I have both face and hands,
And move before your eyes;
Yet when I go my body stands,
And when I stand I lie.

Two bodies have I;
Tho' both join'd in one,
The stiller I stand,
The faster I run.

My sides are firmly lac'd about,
Yet nothing is within;
You'll think my head is strange indeed,
Being nothing else but skin.

Without a bridle or a saddle,
Across a thing I ride and straddle,
And those I ride, by the help of me,
Though almost blind are made to see.

What force and strength cannot get through,
I with a gentle touch can do;
And many in the streets would stand,
Were I not as a friend at hand.

Two little holes in the side of a hill,
Just as you come to the cherry-red mill.

Who are they who fight without weapons
around their lord? The dark ones always
protect him, and the fair ones seek to
destroy him.

(Translated from Old Norse by Kevin Crossley-Holland)

To cross the water I'm the way,
  For water I'm above:
I touch it not, and, truth to say,
  I neither swim nor move.

Creaking, crackling, hard,
Thin and bare its hair,
Hard the skin of its two hands,
Its eyes in the middle of its chest,
And its flesh inside its bones.

(Translated from Gaelic by Alexander Nicolson)

Crooked as a rainbow, slick as a plate,
Ten thousand horses can't pull it straight.

In marble walls as white as milk,
Lined with a skin as soft as silk;
Within a fountain crystal clear,
A golden apple does appear.
No doors there are to this stronghold,
Yet thieves break in and steal the gold.

Thirty white horses on a red hill,
   First they champ,
   Then they stamp,
Then they stand still.

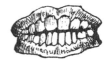

It cannot be seen, cannot be felt,
Cannot be heard, cannot be smelt.
It lies behind stars and under hills,
   And empty holes it fills.
It comes first and follows after,
   Ends life, kills laughter.

J. R. R. TOLKIEN

Voiceless it cries,
Wingless flutters,
Toothless bites,
Mouthless mutters.

J. R. R. TOLKIEN

NONSENSE VERSE

ALARMING SACRIFICE!!

SALE BY AUCTION
ON MONDAY NEXT, APRIL THE FIRST,
OF THE
FURNITURE & EFFECTS
OF
HOOKEY WALKER, Esq.

Consisting of a Glass Bedstead, Iron Feather Bed, a pair of Tin
Sheets, six pounds of Moonshine, three quarts of Pigeons' Milk,
four pounds of the Report of a Gun, three barrels of Roasted Snow,
twelve yards of Sun's Rays, eight Wooden Saucepans, without
bottoms, sides or tops, twelve Spider Web Wine Glasses, three
wings of a Lion, a case of Spiders' Eyebrows, artistically arranged,
six sky-green Shirts, and a decayed New Moon,

A SPLENDID OIL PAINTING
"William the Conqueror Smoking his First Pipe of Tobacco."

a set of Brown Paper Knives and Forks, a Paper Frying Pan, some
Live Butterflies stuffed with Straw, a Policeman's "Move on there!"
(nearly new), the Autograph of the Man in the Moon, and other
articles, too numerous to mention.

Sale to Commence at half-past 5 and 20 minutes past One hour
and a half.

ANON.

THE BOY STOOD ON THE BURNING DECK

The boy stood on the burning deck,
    His feet were full of blisters;
The flames came up and burned his pants,
    And now he wears his sister's.

ANON.

CAPE COD

Cape Cod girls have no combs
They comb their hair with codfish bones

Cape Cod boys they have no sleds
They slide down dunes on codfish heads

Cape Cod doctors have no pills
They give their patients codfish gills

Cape Cod cats they have no tails
They lost them all in sou'east gales.

ANON.

DON'T USE BIG WORDS

In promulgating your esoteric cogitations, or articulating your superficial sentimentalities and amicable, philosophical or psychological observations, beware of platitudinous ponderosity. Let your conversational communications possess a clarified conciseness, a compacted comprehensibleness, coalescent consistency, and a concatenated cogency. Shun double-entendres, prurient jocosity, and pestiferous profanity, obscurant or apparent.

ANON.

WOODEN WHISTLE

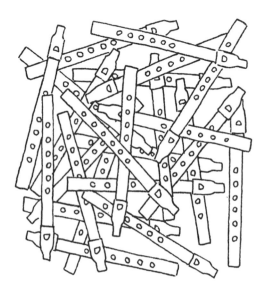

I bought
a wooden
whistle,
but it
wooden
whistle.
I bought
a steel
whistle,
but it
steel
wooden
whistle.
So
I bought
a tin
whistle.
And now
I tin
whistle!

ANON.

JAMAICAN CLAP RHYME

Where your mamma gone?
She gone down town.

She take any money?
She take ten pound.

When your mamma come back,
what she gonna bring back?

Hats and frocks and
shoes and socks.

ANON.

COCOROCOCO-DOODLE-DOO

In Germany Mickey Maus goes KLIRR,
and his dog Goofy yells BAUTZ.
In Spain guns sound JUOOS.
Death-ray pistols kill with a GRRUNG in Sweden.
Snoring Germans sound RUMPEL-KNURR;
a sneeze is HATSCHI;
a loud commotion is RUMS,
and a louder one RUMS-RUMS.

ANON.

235

PRAYER

"Lord! Let me catch a fish
So large that even I,
In telling of it afterwards,
Shall have no need to lie."

ANON.

OF ALL THE . . .

Of all the felt I ever felt
I never felt a piece of felt
That felt the same as that felt felt,
When I first felt that felt.

Of all the ties
I ever tied
I never tied a tie
Like this tie ties.

ANON.

SNAP

One night I saw a little mouse
Come creeping through my door.
I set a trap,
The jaws went 'snap' –
And is my big toe sore!

ANON.

SAY, DID YOU SAY?

Say, did you say, or did you not say
What I said you said?
For it is said that you said
That you did not say
What I said you said.
Now if you say that you did not say
What I said you said,
Then what do you say you did say instead
Of what I said you said?

ANON.

SPRINGFIELD MOUNTAIN

A nice young ma-wa-wa-wa-wan went out to mee-why-wee-why-wo,
To see if he-we-we-we-we could make a she-why-wee-why-wo.

He scarce had mo-wo-wo-wo-woed all round his fee-why-wee-why-
weeld,
When up jump-a come-a rattle come-a snay-way-wake,
and bit him on the he-why-wee-why-weel.

"Now Johnny, dear-why-weer-why-weer, what made you go-wo-wo-
wo-wo
All down in the fee-why-wee-why-weeld, so fur to mo-wo-wo-wo-
wo?"

"Now Sally, mee-why-wee-why-wine, I thought you kno-wo-wo-wo-woed,
The grass was ree-why-wee-why-wipe and had to be mo-wo-wo-wo-
woed."

Then John he dee-why-dee-why-died, gave up the gho-wo-wo-wo-
wost,
And straight to glo-wo-wo-wo-wory he did po-wo-wo-wo-wost.

237

Come all young mee-why-wee-why-wen and warning tay-way-way-
way-wake,
Don't ever get bee-why-wee-why-bit by a poisonous snay-way-way-
way-wake.

ANON.

PROGRESS

I am a sundial, and I make a botch
Of what is done far better by a watch.

HILAIRE BELLOC

SKATEBOARD

My daddy has bought me a skateboard;
  He tried it out first at the store.
And that is the reason why Mummy
  Says Daddy can't walk anymore.

W. R. ESPY

APPRECIATION

Auntie, did you feel no pain
Falling from that willow tree?
Will you do it, please, again?
'Cos my friend here didn't see.

HARRY GRAHAM

CARELESSNESS

A window-cleaner in our street
Who fell (five storeys) at my feet
Impaled himself on my umbrella.
I said: "Come, come, you careless fella!
If my umbrella had been shut
You might have landed on my nut!"

HARRY GRAHAM

POEM IN PRAISE OF PRACTICALLY NOTHING

You buy some flowers for your table;
You tend them tenderly as you're able;
You fetch them water from hither and thither –
What thanks do you get for it all? They wither.

SAMUEL HOFFENSTEIN

SPEL IT RITE

When the witch said
Abradacabra
Nothing happened.
She's a hopeless speller.

ALAN F. G. LEWIS

THE HONEY BEE

the honey bee is sad and cross
and wicked as a weasel
and when she perches on you boss
she leaves a little measle.

DON MARQUIS

THE LONG-SOUGHT-AFTER PROOF THAT MONEY GROWS ON TREES

1. Money is what people get when they sell.
2. Sell sounds the same as cell.
3. A cell is a tiny room.
4. One kind of person who lives in a tiny room is a monk.
5. Monk is a short form of monkey.
6. Monkeys eat bananas.
7. Bananas grow on trees.
   THEREFORE, money grows on trees.

LOUIS PHILLIPS

THE GOLDFISH

The gaping goldfish in his bowl
I'm sure is happy on the whole:
He has that silly vacant look
Because he's never read a book.

A. G. PRYS-JONES

WATER

Water is wet
Fire is hot
I'm me
And you're not.

J. ROSEN

REQUEST NUMBER

Tell me a story, Father, please do;
  I've kissed Mama and I've said my prayers,
And I bade good night to the soft pussy cat
  And the little grey mouse that lives under the stairs.

Tell me a story, Father, please do,
  Of power-crazed vampires of monstrous size,
Of hordes of malevolent man-eating crabs
  And pea-green zombies with X-ray eyes.

G. N. SPROD

THE MODERN HIAWATHA
(from *The Song of Milkanwatha*)

When he killed the Mudjokivis,
Of the skin he made him mittens,
Made them with the fur side inside,
Made them with the skin side outside,
He, to get the warm side inside
Put the inside skin side outside;
He, to get the cold side outside,
Put the warm side fur side inside.
That's why he put the fur side inside,
Why he put the skin side outside,
Why he turned them inside outside.

GEORGE A. STRONG

INDEX
Of Titles and First Lines

THE POETS

AGARD, John (modern, British/Guyanese)
AITKEN, Ian (Aged 12, Canadian)
AMADIUME, Ifi (modern, British/Nigerian)
ANGELOU, Maya (b 1928, Afro-American)
ANTIPATER of Thessalonika
   (398–319 BC, Greek)
ASHONG-KATAI, Selby (Ghanese)
BABURKA, Ilona (modern, American)
BALDWIN, James (1924–1989, Afro-American)
BASHO (1664–1694, Japanese)
BELLOC, Hilaire (1870–1953, Anglo-French)
BERRY, James (b 1925, British/Jamaican)
BI, Shazia (Aged 10, English)
BLAKE, William (1757–1827, English)
BORCHERS, Elisabeth (modern, German)
BOYLE, Bill (modern, English)
BREWSTER, Elizabeth (modern, Canadian)
BRIDGES, Robert (1844–1930, English)
BROWNE, William, (1592–1643, English)
BROWNING, Elizabeth Barrett
   (1806–1861, English)
BROWNING, Robert (1812–1889, English)
BYRON, Lord George (1788–1824, English)
CARROLL, Lewis (1832–1898, English)
CARVER, Raymond (modern, American)
CAUSLEY, Charles (b 1917, English)
CHAMUNORWA, J. M. (b 1924, African)
CHANDIDÁS (14th–15th Century, Bengali)
CHARLIP, Remy (modern, American)
CHAUCER, Geoffrey (1340?–1400, English)
CLARE, John (1793–1864, English)
COATSWORTH, Elizabeth J.
   (1893–1986, American)
COLERIDGE, Samuel Taylor
   (1722–1834, English)
COWARD, Noël (1899–1973, English)
CUSACK, Elaine (Aged 16, English)
DAWBER, Diane (modern, Canadian)
DE LA MARE, John Walter
   (1873–1956, English)
DICKINSON, Emily (1830–1886, American)
DRYDEN, John (1631–1700, English)
DUNDAS, Brenda (Aged 13, Guyanese)
DYLAN, Bob (b 1941, American)
EASTLAKE, William (modern, American)
ENRIGHT, D. J. (b 1920, English)
ESPY, Willard J. (modern, American)
FARJEON, Eleanor (1881–1965, English)
FERLAND, Barbara (b 1919, British/Jamaican)

FROMAN, Robert (modern, American)
FROST, Robert Lee (1874–1963, American)
FULLER, Roy (b 1912, English)
GEORGE, Chief Dan (Co-Salish/Canadian)
GIOVANNI, Nikki (modern, Afro-American)
GOLDSMITH, Oliver (1728–1774, English)
GOODGE, N. T. (Australian)
GRAHAM, Harry (1874–1936, English)
GOULBOURNE, Jean (modern, Jamaican)
GOWAR, Mick (modern, English)
GRAY, Thomas (1716–1771, English)
GRIMES, Nikki (modern, Afro-American)
GUEVARA, Gloria (modern, Nicaraguan)
HALL, Jim (modern, American)
HARDY, Thomas (1840–1928, English)
HARTE, Bret (1836–1902, American)
HIKMET, Nazim (1902–1963, Turkish)
HO, Chih-Chang (659–744, Chinese)
HODGSON, Ralph (1871–1962, English)
HOFFENSTEIN, Samuel (American)
HOLMAN, Felice (b 1919, American)
HOLUB, Miroslav (b 1923, Czech)
HOOD, Thomas (1799–1845, English)
HOPKINS, Gerard Manley
   (1844–1889, English)
HOROVITZ, Michael (b 1935, English)
HORSFORD, Marisa (Aged 12, English)
HUGHES, Langston
   (1902–1967, Afro-American)
HUGHES, Ted (b 1930, English)
HUNTER, Norman (b 1899, English)
IBSEN, Henrik (1828–1906, Norwegian)
JENNINGS, Elizabeth (b 1926, English)
JILL (child, London)
KAYPER-MENSAH, A. W. (Ghanese)
KAZANTZIS, Judith (b 1940, English)
KINSMAN, Jonathan (modern, English)
KIPLING, Rudyard (1865–1936, English)
KIRK, Brian (Aged 11, English)
KLEBECK, William J. (modern, Canadian)
KLEIN, Robin (b 1936, Australian)
KLEOBOULOS (6th Century, Greek)
LAING, R. D. (1930–1990, Scottish)
LANDOR, Walter Savage
   (1775–1864, English)
LANGLAND, William
   (1330–1386, English)
LAWRENCE, D. H. (1885–1930, English)
LEAR, Edward (1812–1888, English)

LEE, Dennis (*b* 1939, Canadian)
LENNON, John (1940–1980, English)
LESTER, Julian (*b* 1939, Afro-American)
LEWIN, Hugh (modern, South African)
LITTLE, Jean (*b* 1932, Canadian)
LIVINGSTON, Myra Cohn
   (*b* 1926, American)
LOWE, Michael (modern, English)
LOWELL, Amy (1874–1925, American)
LUCILIUS (180–102 BC, Ancient Roman)
LYDGATE, John (*c* 1370–1449, English)
MACLEOD, Doug (modern, Australian)
MANDELSTAM, Osip (1891–1938, Russian)
MARK, Sylvia (child, Moosonee/Canadian)
MARQUIS, Don (1878–1937, American)
MASEFIELD, John (1878–1967, English)
MASTERS, Edgar Lee (1868–1950, American)
MAYER, Gerda (*b* 1927, Czech/English)
McCARTNEY, Paul (*b* 1942, English)
McGOUGH, Roger (*b* 1937, English)
McNAUGHTON, Colin (modern, English)
MERRIAM, Eve (*b* 1916, American)
MEW, Charlotte (1869–1928, English)
MIDGLEY, Clare (modern, English)
MILLIGAN, Spike (*b* 1918, English)
MILNE, A. A. (1882–1956, English)
MILTON, John (1608–1674, English)
MITCHELL, Adrian (*b* 1932, English)
MOAGI (Aged 8, South African)
MONRO, Harold Edward (1879–1932, English)
MORRIS, William (1834–1896, English)
MSHAM, Mwana Kupona
   (1810–1860, East African)
NANCY (child, London)
NASH, Ogden (1902–1971, American)
NATT, Maureen (modern, English)
NEZVAL, Vitěslav (1900–1958, Czech)
NIBENEGENESABE, Jacob
   (19th Century, Swampy Cree Indian)
NICHOLS, Grace (*b* 1950, Guyanese)
NOWLAN, Alden (modern, Canadian)
NOYCE, Wilfred (*b* 1918, English)
O'CONNOR, Philip (*b* 1916, Australian)
OWEN, Gareth (*b* 1936, English)
PADDON, Philip (modern, English)
PALIN, Michael (modern, English)
PAPAPETROU, Nicky (modern, English)
PATTEN, Brian (*b* 1946, English)
PÉRET, Benjamin (1899–1959, French)

PRELUTSKY, Jack (*b* 1940, American)
QUINLAND, Linval (modern, English)
REEVES, James (1909–1978, English)
RESTREPO, Edgardo Duran
   (*b* 1948, Colombian)
RICE, John (modern, Scottish)
RICHARDSON, Fred (modern, American)
ROBERTS, Elizabeth Madox
   (1881–1941, American)
ROSEN, Joseph (*b* 1976, English)
ROSEN, Michael (*b* 1946, English)
SANDBURG, Carl (1878–1967, American)
ST JOHN, Justin (modern, English)
SASSOON, Siegfried (1886–1967, English)
SCANNELL, Vernon (*b* 1922, English)
SERRAILLIER, Ian (*b* 1912, English)
SHAKESPEARE, William
   (1564–1616, English)
SHELLEY, Percy Bysshe
   (1792–1822, English)
SHIKIBU, Izumi (10th Century, Japanese)
SIMEON, Lorraine
   (modern, British/Guyanese)
SMITH, Stevie (1902–1971, English)
SÖDERGRAN, Edith
   (1892–1923, Russian)
SOLOUKHIN, Vladimir (*b* 1924, Russian)
SOUSTER, Raymond (*b* 1921, Canadian)
SOUTHEY, Robert (1774–1843, English)
SPENSER, Edmund (1552–1579, English)
SPRINGER, Eintou Pearl (Trinidadian)
STEPHENS, James (1882–1950, Irish)
STEVENSON, Robert Louis
   (1850–1894, Scottish)
STRONG, L. A. G. (1896–1958, English)
SWIFT, Jonathan (1667–1745, Irish)
ŚWIRSZCZYŃSKA, Anna
   (*b* 1909, Polish)
TAGLIAMONTE, Sali
   (Aged 14, Canadian)
TAGORE, Rabindranath
   (1861–1941, Bengali)
TAYLOR, Andrew (modern, English)
TOLKIEN, John Ronald Revel
   (1892–1973, English)
TURNBULL, Gael (modern, English)
VERMA, Shrikant (Indian)
VIORST, Judith (*b* 1931, American)
VIRGIL (70–19 BC, Roman)

WAYMAN, Tom (modern, Canadian)
WHITMAN, Walt (1819–1892, American)
WHITTLE, Robert (modern, English)
WILLIAMS, William Carlos
   (1883–1963, American)
WIDERBERG, Siv (modern, Swedish)
WONG-CHU, Jim
   (modern, Chinese/Canadian)

WORDSWORTH, William
   (1770–1850, English)
WRIGHT, Kit (b 1944, English)
YEATS, William Butler (1865–1939, Irish)
ZOLOTOW, Charlotte (b 1915, American)

SUBJECT INDEX

EXAMPLES OF FORMS, STYLES AND TECHNICAL DEVICES

Note: t=top (poem); m=middle; b=bottom

ACKNOWLEDGEMENTS

The editor and publishers gratefully acknowledge permission to reproduce the following copyright material:

John Agard: 'Don't Call Alligator Long-Mouth Till You Cross River' from *Say It Again, Granny* by John Agard. Reprinted by permission of The Bodley Head Ltd and 'One Question From A Bullet'. Reprinted by permission of the author c/o Caroline Sheldon Literary Agency from *Mangoes and Bullets* (Pluto Press 1985). Ifi Amadiume: 'Bitter'. Reprinted by permission of Karnak House from *Passion Waves* by Ifi Amadiume. Copyright © 1985 by Karnak House. Ancient Egyptian: an excerpt from 'The Satire Of The Trades'. Reprinted by permission of The University of California Press from *Ancient Egyptian Literature* by Miriam Lichtheim. Copyright © 1973–1980 Regents. Anon: 'At Sixty I'. Reprinted by permission of Penguin Books Ltd from *The Greek Anthology* edited by Peter Jay (Allen Lane, 1973). Copyright © Peter Jay 1973. Anon: 'Swarthy Smoke-blackened Smiths'. Reprinted by permission of Penguin Books Ltd from *Medieval English Verse* translated by Brian Stone (Penguin Classics, 1964). Copyright © Brian Stone 1964. Selby Ashong-Katai: 'While Reeds Stand'. Reprinted by permission of The Ghana Publishing Corporation from *A Sonata Of Broken Bones*. Aztec: 'We Mourned For Ourselves' and 'The River Goes By'. Reprinted by permission of Anvil Press Poetry Ltd from *Flower and Song: Poems Of The Aztec Peoples* translated by Edward Kissam and Michael Schmidt, 1977. Basho: 'Winter Downpour'. Reprinted by permission of Penguin Books Ltd from *On Love And Barley: Haiku Of Basho* translated by Lucien Stryk (Penguin Classics, 1985). Copyright © Lucien Stryk 1985. Hilaire Belloc: 'Progress'. Reprinted by permission of The Peters, Fraser & Dunlop Group Ltd from *Sonnets And Verses* by Hilaire Belloc. James Berry: 'Listn Big Brodda Dread, Na!'. Reprinted by permission of Hamish Hamilton Ltd from *Whene I Dance*, Hamish Hamilton 1988. Copyright © James Berry 1988. Bhagavad Gita: extract reprinted by permission of Penguin Books Ltd from *The Bhagavad Gita* translated by Juan Mascaró (Penguin Classics, 1962). Copyright © Juan Mascaró 1962. Shazia Bi: 'City Sights'. Reprinted by permission of the author. Elisabeth Borchers: 'Preparing To Travel'. Reprinted by permission of Anvil Press Poetry Ltd from *Fish Magic: Selected Poems* translated by Annelise Wagner, 1989. Elizabeth Brewster: 'Magnolia Avenue'. Reprinted by permission of Oberon Press, Canada, from *Selected Poems*. Charles Causley: 'My Mother Saw A Dancing Bear'. Reprinted by permission of David Higham Associates Ltd from *Collected Poems* by Charles Causley, Macmillan. J M Chamunorwa: 'The Whirlwind Is Wicked'. Reprinted by permission of The College Press Ltd and J M Chamunorwa from *Poetry in Rhodesia* edited by D E Finn. Chandidás: 'Can Anyone Follow'. Extract reprinted by permission of Unwin Hyman Ltd from *Love Songs Of Chandidás* translated by Deben Bhattacharya. Elizabeth Coatsworth: 'A Lady Comes To An Inn'. Reprinted by permission of Coward-McCann Inc, from *Compass Rose* by Elizabeth Coatsworth. Copyright © 1929 by Coward McCann Inc, copyright renewed © 1957 by Elizabeth Coatsworth. Diane Dawber: 'Contact'. Reprinted by permission of Borealis Press Ltd, Canada, from *Oatmeal Mittens* by Diane Dawber, 1987. Walter de la Mare: 'Mistletoe' and 'The Funeral'. Reprinted by permission of the Literary Trustees of Walter de la Mare and The Society of Authors as their representative from *Collected Rhymes and Verses* by Walter de la Mare. Emily Dickinson: 'A Slash Of Blue'. Reprinted by permission of Little, Brown, USA, from *The Complete Poems Of Emily Dickinson* edited by Thomas H Johnson. Copyright © 1935 by Martha Dickinson Bianchi. Copyright renewed © 1963 by Mary L Hampson. Bob Dylan: 'The Ballad Of Hollis Brown'. Reprinted by permission of the author from *Writings And Drawings*, Jonathan Cape. D J Enright: 'Better Be Kind To Them Now'. Reprinted by permission of Watson, Little Ltd from *Rhyme Times Rhyme*, Chatto & Windus. Eleanor Farjeon: 'Fred' and 'The London Owl'. Reprinted by permission of David Higham Associates Ltd from *Children's Bells*, Oxford University Press and *All The Year Round*, Collins. Kathleen Fraser: 'Wrestling'. Reprinted by permission of Marian Reiner for the author from *Stilts, Somersaults and Headstands* by Kathleen Fraser. Copyright © 1968 by Kathleen Fraser. Robert Froman: 'Graveyard'. Reprinted by permission of the author. Roy Fuller: 'Horrible Things'. Reprinted by permission of Blackie & Son Ltd from *The World Through The Window* by Roy Fuller. Nikki Giovanni: 'Trips'. Reprinted by permission of Farrar, Straus & Giroux Inc from *Spin A Soft Black Song* by Nikki Giovanni. Jean Goulbourne: 'Vida And Ant'. Reprinted by permission of the author and Savacou Publications Ltd from *New Poets From Jamaica*. Mick Gowar: 'Teaching Practice'. Reprinted by permission of Collins Publishers from *So Far So Good*. Harry Graham: 'Appreciation' and 'Carelessness'. Reprinted by permission of Edward Arnold from *Ruthless Rhymes* by Harry Graham. Gloria Guevara: 'The People In Poverty' translated by Peter Wright. Reprinted by permission of Peter Wright. Ho Chi-Chang: 'Written On Return Home'. Reprinted by permission of Hai Feng Publishing Corporation Ltd from *Selected Poems Of The Tang And Song Dynasties* translated by Rewi Alley. Ralph Hodgson: 'The Hammers'. Reprinted by permission of Macmillan, London and Basingstoke, and Mrs Hodgson from *Collected Poems* by Ralph Hodgson. Felice Holman: 'Supermarket'. Reprinted by permission of the author from *At The Top Of My Voice And Other Poems* by Felice Holman, Charles Scribner's Sons, 1970. Miroslav Holub: 'Clowns'. Reprinted by permission of Secker & Warburg from *Notes Of A Clay Pigeon* translated by Jarmila and Ian Milner. Michael Horovitz: 'Growing Up (Concluded?)'. Reprinted by permission of W H Allen from *Growing Up: Selected Poems And Pictures 1951–1979*. Ted Hughes: 'The Stag' and 'O Sing'. Reprinted by permission of Faber & Faber Ltd from *Season Songs* and *What Is The Truth?* by Ted Hughes. Henrick Ibsen: 'Peer Gynt'. Extract reprinted by permission of Penguin Books Ltd from *Peer Gynt* translated by Peter Watts (Penguin Classics, 1966). Copyright © Peter Watts 1966. Japanese Ainu: 'Song Of A Human Woman'.

Reprinted by permission of Princeton University Press from *Songs Of Gods, Songs Of Humans: The Epic Tradition Of The Ainu* edited by D Philippi. Copyright © 1979 by Tokyo University Press. Elizabeth Jennings: 'Wasp In A Room'. Reprinted by permission of David Higham Associates Ltd from *After The Dark* by Elizabeth Jennings, Oxford University Press. Jill: 'Rainbow'. Reprinted by permission of the author and John Scurr School. A W Kayper-Mensah: 'My Hair-Cut'. Reprinted by permission of The Ghana Publishing Corporation from *Proverb Poems*. Judith Kazantzis: 'The Doorman'. Reprinted by permission of the author from *Let's Pretend*, Virago 1984. Jonathan Kingsman: 'Water'. Reprinted by permission of the author. Brian Kirk: 'The Coke'. Reprinted by permission of Blackstaff Press and the author from *The Scrake Of Dawn* edited by Paul Muldoon. Robin Klein: 'Thank-you Letter'. Reprinted by permission of Oxford University Press from *Snakes And Ladders*. Copyright © Robin Klein 1985. Kleoboulous: 'I Am The Maiden'. Reprinted by permission of The University of Chicago from *Greek Lyrics* translated by Richard Lattimore. D H Lawrence: 'Self Pity' and 'Whatever Man Makes'. Reprinted by permission of Laurence Pollinger Ltd and the estate of Mrs Frieda Lawrence Ravagli from *The Complete Poems* edited by Vivian de Sola Pinto, Penguin Books. Dennis Lee: 'Robber J Badguy'. Reprinted by permission of McKnight Gosewich Associates Agency Inc from *Jelly Belly* by Dennis Lee. Lennon/McCartney: 'Blackbird'. Reprinted by permission of International Music Publications. Julius Lester: 'Heroine'. Reprinted by permission of Time Inc Copyright © 1956 Time Inc. Jean Little: 'Pearls'. Reprinted by permission of Kids Can Press Ltd, Toronto from *Hey World, Here I Am!*. Text copyright © 1986 by Jean Little. Myra Cohn Livingston: 'Bessie By Day'. Reprinted by permission of Marian Reiner for the author from *No Way Of Knowing: Dallas Poems* by Myra Cohn Livingston. Copyright © 1980 by Myra Cohn Livingston. Michael Lowe: 'Never Ever Tell'. Reprinted by permission of the ILEA English Centre from *City Lines*. Amy Lowell: 'A London Thoroughfare 2 A.M.' and 'The Fisherman's Wife'. Reprinted by permission of The Houghton Mifflin Company from *The Complete Poetical Works Of Amy Lowell* by Amy Lowell. Copyright © 1955 by The Houghton Mifflin Company. Copyright © 1983 renewed by The Houghton Mifflin Company, Brinton P Roberts Esq and G D'Andelot Belin Esq. Lucilius: 'Mean Old Hermon' translated by Peter Porter. Reprinted by permission of Peter Porter from *The Greek Anthology*, Penguin Books. Colin McNaughton: 'Teef! Teef!'. Reprinted by permission of Walker Books Ltd from *There's An Awful Lot Of Weirdos In Our Neighbourhood* by Colin McNaughton. Copyright © 1987 Colin McNaughton. Osip Mandelstam: 'The Shy Speechless Sound'. Reprinted by permission of Oxford University Press from *Selected Poems* by Osip Mandelstam translated by Clarence Brown and WS Merwin (1973). Copyright © Clarence Brown and WS Merwin 1973. Sylvia Mark: 'Windigo'. Reprinted by permission of Black Moss Press, Canada, from *Children Of The Great Muskeg*. Maurice: 'I Sometimes Lie Reading My Books In Bed'. Reprinted by permission of Barry Mayborg and B T Batsford Ltd from *Creative Writing For Juniors* by Barry Mayborg. Gerda Mayer: '529 1983'. Reprinted by permission of the author. Roger McGough: 'Pets' and 'U.S. Flies In Hamburgers'. Reprinted by permission of The Peters, Fraser & Dunlop Group Ltd. Eve Merriam: 'Pete's Sweets'. Reprinted by permission of Marian Reiner for the author from *Jamboree Rhymes For All Times* by Eve Merriam. Copyright © 1962, 1964, 1966, 1973, 1984 by Eve Merriam. Charlotte Mew: 'Sea Love'. Reprinted by permission of Carcanet Press Ltd from *Collected Poems* by Charlotte Mew. Clare Midgeley: 'Unrolled'. Reprinted by permission of the author. Spike Milligan: 'Goliath'. Reprinted by permission of Spike Milligan Productions Ltd from *Small Dreams Of A Scorpion* by Spike Milligan. A A Milne: 'Rice Pudding'. Reprinted by permission of Methuen Children's Books from *When We Were Very Young* by A A Milne. Adrian Mitchell: 'Bebe Belinda And Carl Columbus'. Reprinted by permission of W H Allen from *Nothingmas Day* by Adrian Mitchell. Moagi: 'When I Am Old'. Reprinted by permission of The Open School, South Africa from *Two Dogs And Freedom*. Harold Monro: 'The Ocean In London'. Reprinted by permission of Duckworth from *Collected Poems* by Harold Monro. Nancy: 'Night Time'. Reprinted by permission of the author and John Scurr School. New Guinea: 'Spider'. Reprinted by permission of Jacaranda Wiley Ltd, Australia, from *Songs of Papua New Guinea*. North American Dakota Indian: 'You Cannot Harm Me'. Reprinted by permission of Penguin Books USA Inc. from *The Portable North American Indian Reader* by Frederick W. Turner III, editor. Copyright © 1973, 1974 by The Viking Press Inc. Brian Patten: 'Burying The Dog In The Garden'. Reprinted by permission of Penguin Books Ltd from *Gargling With Jelly* (Viking Kestrel, 1985). Copyright © Brian Patten 1985. Benjamin Péret: 'Stick No Bills'. Reprinted by permission of Atlas Press from *Remove Your Hat* by Benjamin Péret. Jack Prelutsky: 'There's A New Kid On The Block' and 'My Baby Brother'. Reprinted by permission of Heinemann Young Books from *There's A New Kid On The Block* by Jack Prelutsky. Linval Quinland: 'I Can't Take The Sun No More, Man'. Reprinted by permission of the author and Grasmere School. James Reeves: 'The Intruder'. Reprinted by permission of the James Reeves Estate from *The Wandering Moon And Other Poems* (Puffin Books). Joseph Rosen: 'Water'. Reprinted by permission of the author. Michael Rosen: 'Zoo Cage' and 'My Brother' reprinted by permission of the author. Siegfried Sassoon: 'In The Pink'. Reprinted by permission of George T Sassoon from *The War Poems Of Siegfried Sassoon* edited by Rupert Hart-Davis. Vernon Scannell: 'Hide And Seek'. Reprinted by permission of Vernon Scannell from *Walking Wounded*. Izumi Shikibu: 'On Nights When Hail'. Reprinted by permission of Schocken Books, published by Pantheon Books, a division of Random House Inc from *A Book Of Women Poets From Antiquity To Now* edited by Willis and Aliki Barnstone. Lorraine Simeon: '9 Years Old' and

'Obstacles'. Reprinted by permission of the author. Stevie Smith: 'The River God'. Reprinted by permission of James MacGibbon, the executor, from *The Collected Poems Of Stevie Smith* (Penguin Modern Classics). Edith Södergran: 'The Stars'. Reprinted by permission of Bloodaxe Books Ltd from *Complete Poems* by Edith Södergran, translated by David McDuff (Bloodaxe Books, 1984). Vladimir Soloukhin: 'The Willow'. Reprinted by permission of the author and Stand Magazine. Raymond Souster: 'Summer Shower'. Reprinted by permission of Oberon Press, Canada from *The Collected Poems Of Raymond Souster*. James Stephens: 'The Main-Deep'. Reprinted by permission of The Society Of Authors on behalf of the copyright holder Mrs Iris Wise. Anna Świrszczyńska: 'He Did Not Jump Down From The Third Floor'. Reprinted by permission of Forest Books. Rabindranath Tagore: 'Stray Birds' and 'Vocation'. Reprinted by permission of Macmillan, London and Basingstoke, from *Collected Poems And Plays Of Rabindranath Tagore*. Copyright © 1916 by Macmillan Publishing Company renewed © 1944 by Rabindranath Tagore. JRR Tolkien: 'Teeth', 'Wind' and 'Dark'. Extracts reprinted by permission of Unwin Hyman Ltd from *The Hobbit* by JRR Tolkien. Gael Turnbull: 'A Lamb'. Reprinted by permission of Anvil Press Poetry Ltd from *A Gathering Of Poems, 1930–1980*, 1983. Shrikant Verma: 'Process'. Reprinted by permission of the author and the Indian Council For Cultural Relations, New Delhi, from *Poetry Festival India*. Judith Viorst: 'Night Fun', 'Remember Me' and 'Secrets'. Reprinted by permission of Lescher and Lescher Ltd from *If I Were In Charge Of The World And Other Worries* published by Atheneum, a division of The Macmillan Publishing Group. Copyright © 1981 by Judith Viorst. Virgil: 'An Omen' and 'Snake'. Reprinted by permission of The Hogarth Press on behalf of the executors of the estate of C Day Lewis from *The Aeneid* translated by C Day Lewis. Tom Wayman: 'The Feet'. Reprinted by permission of Harbour Publishing Company Ltd. Barrie Whittle: 'The Whiskers'. Reprinted by permission of the author. Wintu: 'You And I Shall Go'. Reprinted by permission of Farrar, Straus & Giroux Inc from *In The Trail Of The Wind* edited by John Bierhorst. Jim Wong-Chu: 'Ice'. Reprinted by permission of Pulp Press, Canada, from *Chinatown Ghosts*, 1986. Kit Wright: 'Dave Dirt Was On The 259'. Reprinted by permission of Penguin Books Ltd from *Cat Among The Pigeons* (Viking Kestrel, 1987). Copyright © Kit Wright, 1987. Charlotte Zolotow: 'A Dog'. Reprinted by permission of Harper Collins Publishers from *River Winding* by Charlotte Zolotow. Copyright © 1970 by Charlotte Zolotow. Renewed © 1978 by Kazua Mizumura.

While every effort has been made to obtain permission, there may still be cases in which we have failed to trace a copyright holder. The publisher will be happy to correct any omission in future reprintings.